A
LANGUAGE-STUDY BASED ON BANTU

A
LANGUAGE-STUDY BASED ON BANTU

By
F. W. KOLBE

The Black Heritage Library Collection

 BOOKS FOR LIBRARIES PRESS
FREEPORT, NEW YORK
1971

First Published 1888
Reprinted 1971

Reprinted from a copy in the
Fisk University Library Negro Collection

INTERNATIONAL STANDARD BOOK NUMBER:
0-8369-8792-6

LIBRARY OF CONGRESS CATALOG CARD NUMBER:
78-154081

PRINTED IN THE UNITED STATES OF AMERICA

A

LANGUAGE-STUDY BASED ON BANTU

OR

AN INQUIRY INTO THE LAWS OF ROOT-FORMATION,

*THE ORIGINAL PLURAL, THE SEXUAL DUAL, AND
THE PRINCIPLES OF WORD-COMPARISON;*

WITH

Tables Illustrating the Primitive Pronominal System restored in
the African Bantu Family of Speech.

BY THE

REV. F. W. KOLBE,

OF THE LONDON MISSIONARY SOCIETY, FORMERLY OF THE RHENISH
HERERO MISSION ;
AUTHOR OF "AN ENGLISH-HERERO DICTIONARY."

LONDON:
TRÜBNER & CO., LUDGATE HILL.
1888.

𝔅𝔞𝔩𝔩𝔞𝔫𝔱𝔶𝔫𝔢 𝔓𝔯𝔢𝔰𝔰
BALLANTYNE, HANSON AND CO.
EDINBURGH AND LONDON

PREFACE.

THE author, who since 1853 has been a missionary of the London Missionary Society, and before that time was connected with the Rhenish Herero Mission in Damaraland, is, as far as philology is concerned, a self-taught worker. When sent to Damaraland in 1848, he could not possibly have dreamt of ever writing a treatise on the Principles of Language. But when, in conjunction with his colleagues, the Rev. Dr. C. H. Hahn and the Rev. J. Rath, he studied Herero, he was from the very first fascinated with its marvellous structural regularity and wealth of pronominal forms. Fortunately, he knew from Gesenius's Hebrew Grammar and Heyse's Lehrbuch der Deutschen Sprache that there are only three primitive vowels (a, i, u), and was struck to find only these three in the pronominal roots of Herero; and in grouping the formative prefixes of the noun (or roots of pronouns) according to their consonantal sounds, he conjectured that there must be some difference of meaning between such forms as *o*ka- (*KA*), *o*tyi- (*KI*), *o*ku- (*KU*), and that *this difference must be caused by the vowels.* And turning to the verb, he received the same impression, though what that difference might be he had not the remotest conception. So plodding on, he was by degrees led to the discovery of the vowel-laws—laws which are by no means confined to Bantu, but are traceable as well in the roots of

Aryan and other languages. Subsequently, in following up an observation of Mr. Rath's as to the dualistic tendency of the prefix *o*ma- (*a*ma-), the sexual dual became clear to him. Now, these two fundamental principles, viz., the vowel-laws and the sexual dual, have already, at any rate as regards Bantu, met with the approval of two high philological authorities in England, and it is hoped that the other principles set forth in this little work—the result of over thirty years' patient research —will also commend themselves to the student as truths founded on sufficient evidence, and illustrative of the new and fuller light the study of Bantu is destined to shed on the Aryan family and on the origin of language universally. For whilst, in Aryan and other families of speech, the science of language must be content to " begin with roots as its ultimate facts," we are, in Bantu, where we find language in an earlier stage of development, enabled to *discover the very first laws by which language was formed*, and to restore the original concord between language and nature, words and things.

As to material for the study of Bantu, there is a vast deal of it already accessible, as may be seen from the " Index of the Grey Collection," by Dr. Th. Hahn, and the very opportune " Sketch of African Languages," by R. N. Cust, Esq. (Messrs. Trübner & Co.) But still more should be done. The recent opening up of Central Africa and the Congo Regions—all peopled with Bantu nations—should be taken advantage of to collect, with the aid of missionaries and others, the new philological treasures now placed within our reach. And this should be done without delay; for the steady influx of Europeans as time rolls on must necessarily interfere with the primitive purity of the Bantu languages. Would not the Committee of the Imperial Institute take the matter in hand,

and devote a section of the library to African languages, and initiate, at the same time, the compilation of a Comparative Bantu Dictionary ?

"Ever since the publication of the first part of Dr. Bleek's Comparative Grammar," says a leading philologist in a letter to the author, "the importance of the Bantu languages to the scientific study of language has been becoming more and more evident to every comparative philologist." Indeed, strange as it may seem that the science of language should have to go to the Dark Continent for more light, it is nevertheless true that " the origin of the grammatical forms of gender and number, the etymology of pronouns, and many other questions of the highest interest to the philologist, find their true solution in Southern Africa" (Bleek). A single glance at the appended comparative table of pronominal forms ought to suffice to convince the most sceptical of the truth of this.

It is earnestly hoped that the present attempt may, in some measure, contribute towards raising the great Bantu family to the prominent place which it deserves to occupy in the science of language.

F. W. K.

Cape Town,
September 19, 1887.

CONTENTS.

CONTENTS.

CHAPTER IX.

CHAPTER X.

A LANGUAGE - STUDY BASED ON BANTU.

CHAPTER I.

INTRODUCTORY.

WHAT is language? Essays on this ever-recurring question abound : their number is legion. From the earliest times there have not been wanting speculative minds who have endeavoured to solve this problem. Various theories have been propounded, but not one has led to an absolute certainty as to the true beginnings of human speech. Indeed, such is the mass of conflicting opinions on the subject, and such the obscurity which still envelops it, that a Linguistic Society in France is said to declare in one of its first statutes that it will receive no communication concerning the origin of language.

But a resolution like this is evidently premature and unscientific. Is it possible then, in any science or art, to determine beforehand what can be discovered, and what not ? And is it not so that comparative philology is a progressive science, and, compared with other branches of human knowledge, still in its infancy ? What if, after all, in some obscure part of the globe, a language or family of languages be in existence so primitive that the words can be traced to first elements, and that in it the first laws of universal speech can be discovered ?

It appears to me that there is good reason for believing that the African Bantu family, and especially Herero, which may be called the Sanskrit of Bantu, has been preserved in such a primitive state as to make it possible to discover certain simple laws that guided the first man in creating the stock of radicals from which universal

A

language has sprung. Let the student for once divest himself of all preconceived notions on the subject, and carefully examine the facts that shall be laid before him. He will then be convinced that "the continent of Africa supplies new and wondrous forms, the examination of which will upset many favourite theories, based upon the very limited phenomena supplied by the Aryan and Semitic families" (R. N. Cust, "Languages of Africa").

Errors to be noted.—And here, at the outset, I must refer to what for many years has appeared to me to be a fundamental error in our modern science of language. Comparative philologists very frequently confound the terms "isolating" and "monosyllabic." In speaking of Chinese and kindred idioms, they call this class of languages "monosyllabic or isolating, their words being, in fact, composed of simple monosyllabic roots, isolated and, as a rule, independent of each other." And again, "It may be well to state at once that all linguistic systems have passed through this monosyllabic period" (A. Hovelacque). Now, if this be true, if Chinese and other isolating idioms are really monosyllabic, it would be time and strength wasted to resort to an agglutinative and polysyllabic class of languages in search for the elements or ultimate roots of human speech; for nothing can be more certain than the fact that *true* monosyllables have preceded polysyllables in the growth of language. But is it so? are the above-mentioned languages monosyllabic in the true sense of the word? I think it can be proved that they are not; the majority of their respective words have merely been ground down to the *form* of monosyllables, so that they are now pronounced as such, but originally they had more than one syllable. We may, for instance, call the English verbs to "send," to "find," to "bring," monosyllabic words, but then it must be clearly understood that they are not so in reality, but only *pronounced* as such, the wear of time having reduced them to their present defective monosyllabic form. Thus, in speaking of Chinese and kindred idioms, this class of languages ought to be called simply "isolating," or if "monosyllabic" be added, it ought to be explained that by the wear and tear of ages, the bulk of the words in these languages have been reduced to such crippled forms that they have lost their original polysyllabic character, and are at present *pronounced* as monosyllables; as, for example, the Chinese words *kung*, ascend, *tap*, answer, which, like the English *send*, *hang*, had originally two syllables, as they have still in the Swedish *senda* (though here the terminal *a* bears a grammatic character, and is only a substitute for an original *i* or *e*), and Icelandic *hánga*, the consonants *ng* in *kung*, *p* in *tap*, *nd* in *send*, and *ng* in *hang* being remnants of an original second syllable. True monosyllables in Chinese are words like *i*, lean against, depend on, *ki*, lean on one side, *ta*, great, greatly, greatness; but such true monosyllabic forms we also meet with in the agglutinative Herero, as, for example, *pa*, to give, *ta*, to reach, *i*, to go, *ta*, to perish, to die. Words, however, like Chinese *yik*, change, *táp*, tread, *chung*, straight, correct, *hom*, receive, receiver, cavern, were originally dissyllabic, like Herero *tyika*, to be oblique, *yenda*, to go, walk, travel, *ramba*, to chase, pursue, *suta*, to satisfy, pay. In searching for the elements and first laws of human speech, we may find, therefore, as much originality in agglutinative as in isolating languages, since the lexical stock of the latter is not of necessity more primitive than that of the former.

Moreover, the hypothesis that those branches of human speech which present the greatest mechanical difficulty in pronunciation are the most original, is a delusion all the more deceptive for being mixed up with truth; for error is never more dangerous than when it comes to us in the garb of truth. It is unquestionably true that generally those sounds which require the greatest exertion in pronouncing have a claim to priority. Thus, if a word is pronounced in one Bantu dialect *thitha*, and in another *lila*, we know at once that the former pronunciation is nearer the original than the latter. But to assert that those languages whose sounds are most uncouth and clicking, as Hottentot and Bushman, are on that account the most primitive type of speech, is evidently a misapplication of an otherwise sound principle. I doubt whether any linguist would be prepared to accept the Swabian *ischt* as the most original form of Ger. *ist*, Lat. *est*, Skr. *asti*, Eng. *is*.] There cannot be the slightest doubt that Bantu, which had originally no clicks, is, on the whole, much more primitive in form than Hottentot-Bushman.

If it indeed be true that Hottentot, from its very first outset, started with clicks, or, in other words, if clicking phonetics belong to the first stages of root-formation, how is it that, with the exception of the prefixed demonstrative particle in the third person (*xei-*), no clicks are found in that part of speech which in all languages is acknowledged to be the most primitive—the pronoun ? In vain do we look for clicks in such primitive Nama words as TITA, I, saKHUM, we two, saKUM, we, saz, thou, saKHO, you two, saKO, you. This is significant, and tends to show that the so-called clicks are not primitive, but of later growth. There can be little doubt that they originated, after the separation of the several families of speech, in a struggle for existence. When symptoms of decay made their appearance, and the root-words, one after another, began to be reduced to crippled monosyllabic forms, not unfrequently homo-phones, the genius of the language roused itself to fresh exertions, and showed its determination to stem the downward course, and to make itself understood at all hazards. The result was that, besides the introduction of tones, those consonants which were left, especially the gutturals, were often strained to such a pitch that they became what we call clicks. But they remained real consonantal sounds for all that. To show, in Hottentot, how these so-called clicks were employed much in the same way as consonants are in Semitic roots, namely, to act as expositors of different shades of the radical meaning, would not be one of the least interesting studies in African philology. Thus we have, for example, in Nama the verb *uri*, to spring, to jump, and *huri*, to leap; pronounced with the cerebral click *q*, *qhuri*, the same word means to frighten, terrify, properly to frighten up, startle up, " aufscheuchen." And the same principle we notice in the use of the clicks in Kafir. Zulu *hluma* (*hl*=*h*=*k*) is to spring up, shoot up, as plants in spring, to grow well, large; but the change from *hl* to the clicking sound *q* gives the word a different shade of meaning ; for *quma* is to spring up as sparks from the fire, to crack as mealies heated, to start, shiver; whilst a second modification, *gquma*, signifies to throb, as a wound, beat, as a pulse or heart. So it would seem that even the clicks are not excluded from the reign of law.

As an instance how easily a guttural may be turned into a clicking sound, I may mention here, in passing, that once in my hearing a Dutch Cape farmer pronounced the pronoun *gÿ* (you) in a manner which strongly reminded me of the lateral click of the Hottentots. He had never been in contact with clicking tongues, so he did not imitate, like those Boers of whom Barrow remarks—I quote from

Cust's "Sketch of African Languages"—"that they affected similar (clicking) sounds in pronouncing words of their own language."

There is a third error, equally misleading. It is this. Some scholars, in endeavouring to trace a word to its ultimate root, are satisfied if they can only explain the first part, leaving the rest to shift for itself. Thus they derive Latin *pœna*, suffering, punishment, satisfaction, and *purus*, pure, from Sanskrit *pû*, to purify, quite disregarding the undoubtedly radical consonantal element *n* and *r* in these words. Now nothing could be more unsatisfactory. It is, therefore, gratifying to observe that the untenableness of this mode of proceeding has at length been exposed. "If we look, for instance," says Professor Max Müller ("Selected Essays," p. 91), "as I did myself formerly, on such roots as *yudh*, *yug*, and *yaut*, as developed from the simpler form *yu*, then we are bound to account for the modification elements, &c. But what are these modificatory letters? Every attempt to account for them has failed."

Claims of Herero.—Yet we ought not to despair. There is a language still living, more primitive in form than Sanskrit, in which we can trace, in a convincing number of instances, every letter of a word back to its true primitive source. This language is Herero.

Just one or two specimens as an illustration.

The English adverb EKE (A.-Sax. *eac*, Sax. *ôc*, *ac*, O. Fries. *âk*, *oke*, Goth. and Icel. *auk*, Ger. *auch*, Dutch *ook*, Swed. *och*, Dan. *og*) means in addition, also, likewise. It is derived from the verb EKE, to increase, enlarge, extend, add, supply. In A.-Sax. the word has the form *eacan*, and in O. Fries. *aka;* but the majority of the parallel forms, as O. Sax. *ocan*, Icel. *auka*, Swed. *öka*, Dan. *oge*, O. Dutch *oeken*, Lat. *augeo*, Gr. αὔξω, αὐξάνω, all point to *u* as the radical vowel. We may thus accept the Dutch *oeken* and the Icel. *auka* as the most perfect form of the word in Aryan. But farther we cannot go; all we can ascertain in the latter family is, that the root of English *eke* is something like *UK-*, which means to increase, add. In vain do we consult our etymological dictionaries for the reason *why UK-* has that meaning.

Let us see whether we can find a clue in Bantu.

With the above adverb *eke* (*oc*, *oke*, *auk*, &c.) we identify Zulu *onke* or *oke*, Herero *he* (for *uhe*), Konde *ohe*, Tshuana *otlhe* = all, altogether, every one, the whole number, the whole mass, radically identical with the Bantu (Herero) verb *uka* (*yuka*, primitive form *KU-KU*) = to be full : *otyityuma tye uka*, the vessel it (is) full, the literal sense being, as appears in Herero from kindred words of the same genus, the vessel is *running over*. And this meaning it has not by chance, but in accordance with a definite rule, which shall be hereafter stated ; the consonant *k* meaning to run, to go, and the vowel *u* conveying the by-meaning high, upward, over, &c.

We may thus learn in Bantu that the original form of English *eke* is *UKU*, or more correctly *KU-KU*, a reduplication of the monosyllable *KU* (the initial *k* having fallen off), with the primary sense to run upward, to *run over*, to overflow, hence to be full, and to fill, to fill up, increase, add, supply.

Closely allied to EKE (AUK) are the words HUG (O. Eng. *hoge*, *hugge*, Icel. *huga*, to care, think, *hugga*, to comfort, console, Swed· *hägna*, to hedge, wall in, Dan. *hygge*, to guard, A.-Sax. *hegan*, to wall in, guard, Ger. *hegen*, *hägen*, O. Dan. *häge*, to fence, hug, cherish) and HUGE (O. Eng. *hogge*, *houge*, Dutch *hoog* = HIGH, O. Sax. *hoh*, Goth. *háus*, Swed. *hög*, Ger. *hoch*). HUG and HUGE are found close together in the dictionary as near neighbours, but as to origin and meaning they seem to be as distant from each other as the east is from the west. And yet they will probably, by means of the vowel-method (Chapter IV.), one day be recognised as offshoots of one and the same root ; the only difference between them being that in HUGE the vowel *u* means up, *high*, whilst in HUG it has the opposite meaning, from above, from on high, downward, bowed down, hence bent, curved, *round*. The primary meaning of *huge* would seem to be to run up, to be high, whilst *hug* appears to have the radical sense of to run or go round, to enclose, embrace, to surround, as a garden with a fence, a child with the arms. Both words can easily be identified in Herero. Here we have the roots *hunga* and *honga* (nasalised forms of *huka* and *hoka*), which mean—

1. To *go up* (or before), to rise up, be high, end in a point, be prominent ; hence *o-honga*, high point, point, top, and *o-hunga*, isolated hill, properly prominent point ; *hunga-ma* = " sich nach etwas richten," to go by a thing, keep a prominent point in view ; and

2. To *go down*, bow, bend, curve, go or be round, go round a

thing, put something round it ("umstellen"), protect, as with a fence, cover, thatch, &c. (*hok-era*); take care of, "pflegen, verpflegen," nourish, foster, cherish (*hunga*).

Now, if the above identification is true, then we are able to trace in Bantu the very first monosyllabic origin of HUGE and HUG. For in Herero the root-words *huka, hoka,* strengthened *hunga, honga,* can be proved to be modifications of *kuka,* to rise, start, travel, and *koka,* to be crooked, curved. The primitive monosyllabic root is *KU,* reduplicated *KU-KU = HU-KU = HU-NGU =* to *go up* (be high, foremost, prominent), and to *go down* (bow, bend, curve, put round).

Or let us take the verb to SEND, A.-Sax. *sendan,* Goth. *sandjan,* O. H. Ger. *santjan, sentjan,* N. H. Ger. *senden,* Dutch *zenden,* Icel. *senda,* with which we identify Herero *hinda* or *shinda* (to send), allied to Goth. *sinth,* O. H. Ger. *sind,* A.-Sax. *sidh,* way, journey, and to Herero *tyinda* (*kinda*), to go out, remove, travel.

According to Bopp, the primary meaning of Goth. *sandjan* is to cause to go, "ich sende, mache gehen" ("Vocalismus," p. 216). But a comparison with the identical forms in Bantu enables us to put the sense in a more definite shape; to *send* means primarily to cause to go *out,* to make go from within one place to another, "ausgehen machen." The first vowels, *a* and *e,* in *sandjan* and *send* are substitutes for a primitive *i,* which gives a root the by-meaning *in* and *from within* or *out.* This is very plain in Herero. Indeed, it is not always the vowel *a* that can be looked upon as most primitive in an Aryan group of roots in which several vowels compete. Herero *hinda* or *shinda* (to *send*) is the parallel *i*-form of *kanda,* to go or run together, congeal, and *kunda,* to go or run over, be full, and its literal meaning is to *make go out,* whilst the cognate *tyinda* (*kinda*) signifies to *go out,* leave a place, travel as nomads, hence also to carry a burden. The A.-Sax. *sendan* is, therefore, nearer the original (*KINDI* or *KHINDI*) than the Goth. *sandjan.* In the Aryan words *sinth, sind, sidh,* way, journey, which correspond to Herero *tyinda,* Zulu *sinda* (be burdened, heavy, properly travel, carry a burden), the primitive *i* has been preserved.

In Zulu the two Herero verbs *tyinda* (Aryan *sind*) and *hinda* (Eng. *send*) have coalesced in the one form *sinda,* which means in that idiom—

    a. (to *go out,* to outgo, outrun), exceed, reach beyond ;

    b. (to *go out*), go out free, escape, get off, as from a punish-
ment, escape from an illness, get restored to health, be
saved, healed ;

    c. (to *go out,* leave a place, as nomads, carry a heavy burden),
be heavy, weigh down, oppress with weight ;

    d. (to *go out,* do as in removing, take all the things out, clear
out a native hut, in order) to smear the earthen floor with
fresh cow-dung (*sinda* being in this case used jocularly,
the clearing out of the hut preceding the smearing being
compared to an exodus).

In Tshuana the root has assumed the form of *sita* (= *sinda, nd*
being in this dialect frequently hardened to *t*), which means (to outgo,
outrun), overcome ; causative *sitisa* (outrun, outdo), exceed, surpass.
The identical *sidi* in Hausa denotes (to go out, leave, remove, hence)
to bear, carry, endure.

The study of Bantu enables us thus to demonstrate that the
primary meaning of *send* is to (cause to) *go out.*

But we can go even farther than this. We can analyse Herero
hinda (*hindi* = *KINDI* = *KI-TI, i*-form of the genus K*a*-T*a*) and
reduce it to its two monosyllabic elements K*a* and T*a*, both of which
still exist in Bantu as independent true monosyllabic words—KA
meaning to move, to run, to go, and TA to stretch, reach, extend, a
combination of which we have in

Ka-Ta

    = move-stretch (the legs, feet) = step, go, run, hence

kata = go close *together,* stick to ;—nasalised
kanda = go or run *together,* congeal ; one of the *i*-forms being
hinda (*KINDA*) = (cause to) go *out,* send.

All this will be clearer hereafter, when the laws and beginnings
of primitive speech are treated.

Fundamental Philological Truths.—I shall now proceed to state in
a few brief theses some truths bearing upon the origin of language
which, I believe, are discoverable in Herero.

I.

Language is the offspring of sight, not of sound. The ground-work of language was not formed in imitation of the cries of animals, nor were the first articulate sounds of an interjectional nature accidentally uttered, but roots were produced by rational observation guided by definite laws—laws *founded on the beautiful harmony between the three motion-aspects in nature* (life-motion, wind-motion, rest) *and the three organs of speech* (guttural, labial, dental), as will be explained hereafter. ,Names like *cuckoo, pewit,* formed in imitation of sound, and interjections as *pooh, pshaw,* are few in number, and do not belong to the organism of language.

II.

The beginnings of language consist. of true monosyllables, with one consonant and one vowel, such as *KA, TI, PU,* with wide and general meanings, as to move, to go, to stretch, to wave, to fly. Words ending with a consonant, as, for example, Chinese *tap, hom,* are mutilated forms, and though at present *pronounced* as mono-syllables, they are not such in reality.

III.

By far the greatest number of roots in all languages (the isolating not excepted) are combinations of two primitive monosyllables which in most languages have lost the terminal vowel, as Chinese *yi-k',* Eng. *fi-nd', loo-k', rea-d',* which, however, in Bantu have been preserved in their complete form, as *ra-nda,* buy, *hi-nga (hi-ngi),* drive, *mu-na (mu-nu),* see. No true primitive root ever exceeds two syllables.

IV.

The two first grand principles of language are *motion* (associated with rest) and *space,* the consonants representing motion (and the absence of motion or rest), and the vowels the various relations as to space, (time), and locality. The primeval laws which regulated in the beginning the use of the primitive consonants (guttural, dental, labial) and the primitive vowels (*a, i, u*) can still be observed in Herero.

V.

The differences between the several families of speech are, on the whole, not radical or material, but merely grammatical, formal, and conventional, each family having moulded what it possessed of the original common stock in its own fashion.   The vowel-method (see Chapter IV.) will enable the science of language to demonstrate the origin of the several families of speech from one common source.

CHAPTER II.

PRIMITIVE ALPHABET—PRIMEVAL LAWS OF CONSONANTS.

LANGUAGE, like every other "good and perfect gift, cometh from above, from the Father of lights." But it must not be forgotten that reason is a gift even greater than language. God did not give language to man as He imparted to the nightingale her stereotyped inimitable music, but He gave him more; He endowed him with reason and the organs of speech, and thus enabled him to *create* language. Man is the image of God; language, in more than one aspect, the image of man. Very true is Herder's remark that the origin of language is really divine, inasmuch as it is human. The nature and measure of immediate divine assistance which Adam received in respect to language must of course remain a mystery; but so much is plainly revealed in Scripture that the giving of names to animals was the work not of the Creator, but of the first man. "And out of the ground," we read (Gen. ii. 19, 20), "the Lord God formed every beast of the field, and every fowl of the air; and brought them unto Adam to see what *he* would call them : and whatsoever Adam called every living creature, that was the name thereof. And Adam gave names to all cattle, and to the fowl of the air, and to every beast of the field." Now in this way, surrounded by the endless variety of the animal creation, Adam practised language, and created those root-words which are still in the mouth of his children to this very day. Those who hold that Adam was created with a perfect philosophical language, do not consider that the intellectual labour of creating language with its accompanying daily discoveries and joys, must have greatly cheered our first parents in their solitude, and that, therefore, we have to look upon that task as a great boon bestowed on them by a loving and all-wise

Creator. But enough. It is a fact which can be demonstrated that the present grand structure of human speech arose by intelligent effort, and in accordance with certain simple laws, from small, very small beginnings; and this fact, as it is in keeping with all the works of God, is also, like every other fact in true science, in perfect harmony with Revelation.

Primitive Alphabet.—The primitive language would appear to have commenced with seven sounds, represented in the following scheme:—

From these principal letters evolved the aspirates or stronger sounds, *kh, tl, ph,* and, on the other hand, the medial or softer sounds, *g, d, b,* and the rest of the consonantal sounds down to the phantastic phonetic excrescences of Hottentot and Bushman. The great variety of vowel-sound can, as is well known, be traced back to the three primary vowels *a, i, u,* the pronunciation being as in German and Italian.

The vowel *a* corresponds to the guttural *k;* *i* to the dental *t;* and *u* to the labial *p.*

Primeval Consonantal Laws.—The guttural *k* (*ka*) is the representative of breath, life, and spontaneous motion; *t* (*ti*) means death, absence of motion, rest, hence also stretching, reaching; and *p* (*pu*) is the natural and legitimate interpreter of wind, air, and motions caused by the wind or observed in the air, as the waving motion of the wings of a flying bird or the branches of trees.

The letter *m* is unique; only in the primitive noun (Bantu prefix and pronoun) it seems to be original, its meaning being mother, female, partner, mate, and, transferred to localities, inner, hence also present, place, properly mother, womb, cavern, grotto, house. In verbs, *m* will be found, in most cases, to be a substitute for an original *p,* as, for example, in Herero *kama,* press together, squeeze out, *tama,* stretch, *pama,* compress; words which are contractions respectively of *kamba* (*KA-M-PA*), *tamba* (*TA-M-PA*), and *pamba* (*PA-M-PA*).

Examples.—The following examples from Herero and Zulu will illustrate the powers of the consonants of the three different organs. The form in italic capitals is the approximate primitive one.

K

h, sh, s, hl, ty, y, g, ng, dy, &c.

kauka (Zulu), *KA(-uka)*, come to a stop, be broken off, interrupted, be stayed, as blood, lit. run back, be checked in running (*kauka* being the inversive form of the obsolete *ka*, to run). Parallel transitive form :

kaula, KA(-ula), bring to a stop, terminate, put an end to, set a bound or limit to, staunch, as blood, lit. counteract running, stop running ;

i (Herero), *KI*, to go, to go out ;

u (Bantu), *KU* (pron.), he, she, properly the erect walking being, man ;

kaka (Bantu), reduplication of *KA*, in Zulu bitter, pungent, properly hard, as in *imi-kaka* (hardened) rings of a tree; in Herero to become dry, hard, as a healing wound, to get a crust, the literal sense being to run together, congeal, become hard, or run on the ground, harden (the ground), beat a (hard) road.

tyika (Herero), *KI-KI*, run out of the straight line, be oblique, slanting ;

kuka (H.), *KU-KU*, (run upward, start up), start for a trip, go on a journey, travel ;

kanga (H.), *KA-KA*, smoke, fumigate thoroughly, properly make dry, hard, as fumigated meat : literal meaning, like *kaka*, to run on the ground, to harden, or to run together, congeal, (hence in Zulu *kanga*, draw or attract the eyes, look well, be attentive, watch, make the eye strong, hard), allied to Herero *nyanga* in *nyangatara*, to swarm, crowd, be numerous, properly run together for sight-seeing, as a crowd, the word being compounded of *nyanga*, run together, collect, crowd, and *tara*, look, see ; *kangama* (Herero), raise oneself, as in getting up from sleep, make oneself strong, properly hard ; frequentative form *kangura*, to burn, properly harden, bricks ;

hanga (H.), *KA-KA*, to assemble, get together, collect, as people, warriors, properly make run together;

tyenga (H.), *KI-KI*, frequentative form *tyengura*, to upset, as a pot containing food, lit. cause to run out, throw out (the contents of a pot);

henga (H.), *KI-KI* (run out of the way, shift, turn aside, *i.e.*), change;

kunga (H.), *KU-KU*, run upward from the stomach, vomit.

T

th, z, s, d, nd, r, l, n, &c.

ta (Herero), to stretch, to reach;

ta (H.), to die, to perish;

tata (H.), to throw on the ground, to lay prostrate, properly stretch as a dead one, on the ground;

tandaura = *tandavara* (H.), to stretch, extend, from *tanda*, *TA-TA*, to stretch;

rara or *lala* (Bantu), *T'A-TA* or *DA-DA*, stretch (originally on the ground), lie down, sleep;

tiza (H.), *TI-TI*, prop up, support, lit. place a dead thing, as a post or a stone (*e-tize*, a prop) against a house, a wall, in an oblique position; a kindred form being

teza (H.), *TI-TI*, to follow in a track, to pursue, properly to over-take, stop progress, bring to a stand, hold back, as a prop, a tottering wall, analogous to Lat. *sustineo*, to hold up, support, but also oppose, restrain; allied to *tiza* and *teza* is

tila (Tshuana), *TI-TI* or *TI-DI*, to avoid, get out of the way of anything likely to harm, turn aside, identical with Herero *tira*, to fear (be kept back by something);

tola (Zulu), *toora* (Herero), *TU-TU* or *TU-DU*, to pick up, take up (orig. lift up something lying on the ground), carry away;

lula (Z.), in *lulama*, *TU-TU* or *DU-DU*, rise up a little from a recumbent position, properly lie up, sit up (Tshuana), stretch upward; in Herero (*rurama*) be straight, erect;

tundura (H.) = *tutumuna*, *TU-TU*, raise, lift up, as one in a fainting fit;

in-tondo (Z.), *TU-TU*, heap of (dead things, as) stones, money, grain.

P

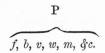

f, b, v, w, m, &c.

pa (Bantu), give, primarily make grasp, cause to take with the fingers, stretch the hand, fingers, the finger-rows being in Bantu looked upon and treated as wing-like objects ;

papa (Zulu), flutter, fly as a bird : **u**-*pape*, a wing, a plume ;

vava or *papa* (Herero), in *vavera, papera, PA-PA*, to spread out, as a skin on the ground (originally to spread out the wings) ;

pepa (Z.), *PI-PI*, start (properly fly) suddenly aside, evade, escape by starting aside ;

pepa (H.), *PI-PI*, blow, as in making fire : *om-bepo*, wind ;

pemba (H.), *PI-PI*, be smooth, pure, properly bright, shining, burning, blown, stirred, as fire ;

pema (H.), contracted from *pemba*, to blow the nose ;

pupa (H.), *PU-PU*, to flow, properly drive on the water, buoy up, be light, as a wing, feather ;

pupa = pumba (H.), *PU-PU*, to prune, lop (properly lighten) a tree.

As to the pronominal roots or prefixes of the noun, here too the working of the consonantal laws can still be traced in Bantu. In offering the following Herero nouns as illustrations, let me premise a brief remark on the meanings of some of the prefixes occurring in them. It will guard us against confusion and misunderstandings.

The prefix *oku-* xv. in such nouns as *oku-tui*, ear, &c., is different in character from the infinitive *oku-*. The former is a true prefix, but the latter is merely the preposition or directive *ku* (= to) elevated to the rank of a prefix. Both are indeed radically one, but the difference is that the *oku-* in *oku-tui* is a true primitive noun and personal prefix, whilst the *oku-* of the infinitive is a secondary form. Thus *oku-tui* (*oku-THUVI*), ear, is properly the hearing person, or the hearing one, *i.e.*, ear, but *oku-zuva* (*oku-T'HUVA*) means literally "the to hear" (infinitive) or "hearing."

In the *e*-**v** (or *e*-) class, two (or three) classes of nouns have coalesced which are diametrically opposed to each other. There we have, first of all, e-(*KA*) for living, and then e-(*TI*) for dead things. Also in *o*u- xiv. some classes are thrown together: the singular (*PU*), the plural (*KHU*), and perhaps another plural form (*PHU*). As to the prefix *o*zon- x., it is sometimes a true plural, as in *o*zon-*gombo*, goats, plur. of *o*n-*gombo*, goat, and might then be distinguished as *o*zo-*n*- (*KHA-KIMI*), but in nouns like those we shall quote presently, it is one of the forms of the sexual dual, *o*zon- (primit. form *TI-MI*, *TU-MU*).

K = living being or thing :

*o*mu-*ndu* (*KU-MU-ndu*), man (orig. human couple) ;

*o*n-*nyanda* (*KI-MI-nyanda*), cattle, properly cattle-pair ;

*o*n-*gombe* (*KI-MI-kombe*), ox or cow (orig. ox and cow) ;

*o*n-*yama* (*KI-MI-yama*), flesh (orig. suckling animal, " säugethier," animal whose meat may be eaten) ;

*o*m-*bua* (*KI-MI-bua*), dog (male and female dog) ;

*o*n-*gombo* (*KI-MI-kombo*), goat (he- and she-goat) ;

*o*n-*du* (*KI-MI-zu*), sheep (ram and ewe) ;

*o*n-*geama* (*KI-MI-keama*), lion (and lioness), and most other animals.

*o*ku-*oko*, arm, front-leg, *o*ma-*oko* (*KA-MA-oko*), arms, properly male-female-arm, both arms ;

*o*ku-*rama*, leg, *o*ma-*rama* (*KA-MA-rama*), (both) legs ;

*o*ku-*tui*, ear (as being fleshy, living, or moving, pricked up, as the ear of an animal), plural (orig. sexual dual) *o*ma-*tui* (*KA-MA-tui*), (both) ears ;

e-*ke* (*KA-ke*), hand, *o*ma-*ke* (*KA-MA-ke*), hands, originally male-female hand, right and left hand ;

e-*vere* (*KA-vere*), female breast, *o*ma-*vere* (*KA-MA-vere*), breasts (orig. the two breasts, looked upon, as all fleshy members of the body, as living).

T = dead thing :

e-*yo* (*TI-yo*), tooth. The Zulu *i*-zin-*yo*, dialectic *i*-tin-*yo*, is the sexual dual *TI-MI-yo* = male-female-row of teeth, or the two rows of teeth, abbreviated in-*yo* ;

e-*tupa* (*TI-tupa*), bone ;

e-ue (*TI-ue*), stone ;

*o*zon-*yara* (*TI-MI-yara* or *TU-MU-yara*), (double row of finger) nails, Zulu (*iz*)in-*tipo*, nails, singular *u*(lu)-*tipo* (*TU-tipo*) ;

*o*zon-*ya* (*TI-MI-ya* or *TU-MU-ya*), horns (properly pair of horns), Zulu *i*(z)im-*pondo*, horns, sing. *u*(lu)-*pondo* (*TU-pondo*) ;

*o*zom-*bumbu* (*TU-MU-pumbu*), eyebrows, properly the pair of eyebrows (r. *pumba*, to prune, to lop, to clip, from the shortness of the hair), sing. oru-(*p*)*umbu* (*TU-pumbu*), and also, but irregularly, *om-bumbu ;*

oru-*uua* (*TU-uua*), rock ;

oru-*uma* (*TU-uma*), dust.

P = waving thing :

*o*u-*ta* (*PU-ta*), bow (*PU* = wing, branch, bough, tree, &c.) ;

*o*mu-*ti* (*PU-MU-ti*), tree (from the branches resembling a pair of wings) ;

*o*mu-*nue* (*PU-MU-nue*), finger, lit. the waving pair, the two finger-rows, on account of their being like the wings of a bird or the branches of a tree ;

*o*mu-*na* (*PU-MU-na*), lip, originally the waving, flapping, or blowing pair, their motion being like that of the eyelids or wings ;

*o*mu-*pepo* (*PU-MU-pepo*), bellows, lit. the blowing lips ;

*o*mu-*kova* (*PU-MU-kova*), skin, cover, orig. probably pair of wings : *omukova u'eho*, eyelid, cover of the eye, properly male-female-wing of the eye (-pair) ;

*o*mi-*tuka*, levity, plur. of *o*mu-*tuka* (*PU-MU-tuka ;* r. *tuka*, to start up, to fly up), orig. probably pair of wings ;

*o*mu-*vare* (*PU-MU-vare*), large sheet of water, lake, lit. the wing-like waving expanse (-*vare* = wide, expanded) ;

*o*mu-*ramba* (*PU-MU-ramba*), torrent, lit. chasing, pursuing lake (r. *ramba*, follow after, pursue) ; Kafir *u*m-*lambo ;*

*o*mu-*pupo* (*PU-MU-pupo ;* r. *pupa* = to flow), stream, torrent (from the motion of the waves).

From specimens like the above, which abound in Bantu, we arrive, by the safe method of induction, at the following general principles in the domain of the consonants :—

   1. Every *living* being and thing (man and animal kingdom), and

B

all spontaneous motion, is represented by the *breathing* throat-letter *k* and kindred gutturals and palatals.

2. Every *dead* thing (including the mineral kingdom), and all absence of motion or rest, is expressed by what may be called the *dead* or tooth-letter *t* (it being produced by contact of the tongue with the *dead* rows of teeth), and other dentals and linguals, though, as we have shown, dentals and linguals are also, under certain conditions, applied to indicate motions.

3. Every *waving* thing (vegetable kingdom, &c.), and all waving motion, and the blowing action of the wind which causes it, is denoted by the blowing lip-letter *p* and other labials.

This natural correspondence between Thing and Word is, of course, to a great extent obliterated in our modern languages. But even in the most developed, traces are left to show that originally it existed. With the addition of the word " originally," the following quotation from Trench's " Study of Words " (p. 29) appears to me true and to the point : " The words which we use are (originally) not arbitrary and capricious signs, affixed at random to the things which they designate, for which any other might have been substituted as well, but they stand in a real relation to these."

Reasons for the Consonantal Laws.—These are self-evident, as we have intimated just now ; for no articulation could have been a better representative of breath, life, and spontaneous motion than the consonantal sound *ka* (and its modifications), which is produced by the tongue touching the soft palate in closest contact with the fountain of breath or the throat, and aided by the breath from the throat. I am aware that the appellation " guttural " for *k* is objected to by some, who prefer to speak of it as a palatal, restricting the term " guttural " to the stronger and harsher modifications of *k*, as we find them in Hebrew and other languages. But we are not dealing here with an artificial alphabet, but with the "alphabet of Nature ; " and it is not likely that any one will contend that the sound *ka* was pronounced by primeval man merely by bringing the tongue to the palate, *without at the same time emitting breath from the throat.* In pronouncing *ti* and *pu* we can very well dispense with the throat, but we cannot say *ka* in a natural manner without the sound being accompanied by emission of breath. As to the dental *ti*, produced as this sound is by contact of the tongue with a

double row of dead, hard objects, its fitness for describing the absence of motion, hardness, death, &c., is obvious. Nor will it be denied that the choice of the lip-letter *p* (and its modified sounds) for expressing the notion of blowing, waving, flying, was the most simple and natural that could have been made. Indeed, there was no choice at all in the matter. If in any degree we succeed in bringing ourselves to look at God's beautiful world as if we saw it, like the first man, for the first time, our very first observation will be the threefold variety in reference to motion, namely, spontaneous motion (men, animals, living members of the body), waving motion (wings, branches, plants, waves of the ocean, lakes, and rivers, the eyelids, lips, &c.), and the absence of motion (teeth, bones, earth, stones, metal, &c.); and we shall then be struck at the same time with the corresponding fitness of the representatives of the three organs of speech: of *ka* to make breath, life, and voluntary motion audible; of *pu* to turn wind, air, and the waving motions therein into articulate sound; and of *ti* to be the audible sign for the absence of motion, dead matter, solidity, and rest. *It is out of this intimate union of the threefold motion-aspect in Nature and the three corresponding organs of speech that Language was born.*

All this will appear to some, I am afraid, as a mere play of fancy. But let it be remembered that the element of imagination figures as an important factor in the creation of language. We who are living in an advanced state of culture find it difficult to realise the primitive simplicity, *naiveté*, and even poetry of the world when it was young. It has been said that the last man who leaves this world will be a poet: be this as it may, it is certain that the *first* man was, and the immortal poem he produced is Language. In researches like those we are now engaged in, on the sacred paradisiacal ground of the origin of language, we must stoop down, and in a literal sense put off the shoes from off our feet; for how can we otherwise discover that our feet, on account of the rows of toes, are wing-like objects? We may smile now at such an idea, but it was in that light that the hands with the finger-rows and the feet with the rows of toes appeared to our first parents. Some time ago I listened with pleasure to an able lecture "on wings," in which the lecturer also called attention to man as a *winged being*, confining his remarks, of course, to the soaring mental powers of man; and it is not likely that any one of his hearers did find fault with him for not discovering wings among the members of the human body.   It would, however, have been different, I am inclined to think, if the lecture had been addressed to the first family of man ; for they would have considered it defective on the ground that no mention was made at all of the wing-like members of the body, viz., the finger-rows, the rows of toes, the pair of eyelids, and the pair of lips.   Now, it is this primitive intuition of Nature which we must strive to get restored, if we would arrive at clear and true ideas regarding the origin of language.

CHAPTER III.

PRIMEVAL LAWS OF THE VOWELS.

THE vowel-sounds had, in the beginning of language, an inherent power to modify the sense of a root, forming in this way from a single root a whole cluster of independent root-words, with one pervading general idea, but differing as to space and locality. As the consonants represent, regulate, and diversify motion, so the vowels are originally signs for the various positions and relations in space. These relations—as, for example, far, together, on the surface, within, without, in, between, aside, oblique, up, on high, over, through, &c.—at present denoted by prepositions and adverbs of place (or space), were originally indicated by the three primary vowels *a, i, u.*

If, therefore, *KA* signified to run on the ground, to run together, the meaning of *KI* was to run in, or from within, out, to run in or between, aside, out of the straight line, oblique, and *KU* conveyed the sense of running upward, on high, over, and from above, downward, also ahead, before, &c.

It is, therefore, wrong to say that "the vowel *a* is *the* great primitive vowel," and " that if an *a*-sound compete with another vowel-sound, the *a*-sound belongs to the primitive form." We may, indeed, assign to the vowel *a* the honourable place of being first among equals, but farther we cannot go; for it can be proved that the other two vowels, *i* and *u*, are equally primitive, and quite independent of *a*. Each of the three primary vowels has a distinct individuality, moves in a sphere exclusively its own, and performs its own peculiar functions.

A.

The vowel *a* gives a root the by-meaning—

on or along the ground, on the surface,
flat, level, horizontal,

near the ground, not raised, not vertical, high, or full-grown, hence
diminutive, common, low, small (in pronominal roots),
wide, broad, extended, stretched out,
abroad, far, distant,
there, absent, past (in pronominal roots),
straight, in a line, parallel with,
together, toward, at—and the reverse,
asunder, scattered, spread.

Any action, motion, or condition naturally inciting a horizontal
gesture with one or both arms, falls within the sphere of *a*.

I.

The vowel *i* signifies—

in, inner, inside, hidden,
in a place, present, here (in pronominal roots),
within—and from within,
out, without, outside, out of, forth,
out(running), exceeding (in length or height, be big, tall), excelling,
        projecting, straight, stiff,
(running) out (as liquids, hence also) over, up,
out of the way, at the side, aside, to and fro, turning, circling,
out of the straight line, oblique, across, athwart,
in, between.

U.

The vowel *u* has the power of pointing upward to motions and
actions in the air which would call forth, as a natural gesture, the
lifting up of the arm.   *U* means—

above the ground, in the air,
up, upward, vertical, perpendicular,
high, over,—hence, as over a river,
through,
overflowing, full,
before, in front, ahead—and the opposite,
at the back, behind, following another,
up, erect,
rising, great, large,
above—and from above,

downward, down, under, below,
bowed down, bent, curved, round, crooked, twisted.

These primeval powers of the vowels, therefore, naturally produce a great variety of meaning in one and the same radical. So we find, for example, in Hebrew, that the meanings to cry, call, to be astir, awake, to dig, hollow out, to go round, encircle, enclose, and several others are all centred in the one form GHUR: the reason is because the consonantal skeleton of the root, *GHR,* means "to go," and the vowel *u* gives it the by-meaning of (1) upward, hence to go up, rise, and rouse, cry, call, awake, and be awake; (2) to go from above, downward, bow down, bend, curve, go round, hence to encircle or enclose; but also (3) to hollow out, dig, properly go round with a digging instrument, as in widening a hole, make a round hole. Now the same meanings are combined in Herero KORA. This verb means (1) to go up, rise up, run over and make run over, fill, feed up, nurse, as an infant, make grow; (2) to go round, as in a round native hut, when searching for something; and (3) to go round with an instrument, hollow out. Nor shall we have to go far in looking for an example in our own languages: the Aryan root *KUR (K.RU, K.RO, G.RO,* &c.) at once presents itself for illustration. The vowel *u* (*o*) gives *KR* (*GR*) the by-meaning of (1) upward, up, high, in GRO*w,* Dutch GROE*ien,* and in GREA*t,* Ger. GRO*sz,* Dutch GRO*ot;* (2) from above, downward, bowed down, bent, curved, as in Lat. CUR*vo,* to CROO*k,* allied to Ger. KRU*mm,* Dutch KRO*m;* hence (3) round, hollowed out, hollow, in CRO*ck,* CRU*se,* Dutch, KROE*s,* KRU*ik,* Swed. KRU*ka,* Ger. KRU*g,* Gael. CRO*g* (the round, hollow thing, earthen vessel), not to mention a number of other words sprung from the same root.

But it will, of course, not be expected that in all cases the primitive vowels should have retained their original purity; *a,* in a number of roots, has become *e; i,* too, often sounds like *e;* and not less frequently do we find *u* changed into *o.* Nay, more than this. There are rare instances in Bantu in which a radical *u* has changed to *e* or *a;* for example, Zulu *tamba,* to subdue, be tame, soft, mild, gentle, which evidently is a modified form of the original *tumba,* to bring into submission, take captive, capture, just as the identical English, *to tame* (Lat. *domo*), is a variation of the (as far as the radical vowel is concerned) more primitive *doom* (O. H. Ger. *tuomjan*), the primary sense being in both words the same, namely, to make go down, to bow down, to subdue (as animals, enemies), hence also to pronounce judgment upon captives of war, decree, punish, condemn. Similar cases of vowel-shifting will be often met with in the Aryan languages, though here the radical vowels have, on the whole, stood their ground much better than in the Semitic and Hamitic languages, Hottentot-Bushman included, where the radical vowel-element has been terribly convulsed. Nevertheless, even in the latter families the working of the primeval vowel-laws can still be traced.

We have, for example, in Hottentot (Nama)—

xkua (for *XKUNA*, to go up, to rise), to dawn ; and the reverse
xkuâ (for *XKUNA*, to go from above, down), to descend, to come
　　(properly bow) down (*xkuâ-gha*) ; from this
xkuâ-p (*XKUNA-P*, the bending one, or) the knee ;
quni (the bending one), the elbow ; cf. Herero *e-kono* (the bending
　　one), the arm, hence also branch ; and Gr. γόνυ, Eng. *knee*
　　(the bending one) ;
vkona (to stoop low, crouch), to beg ; *cona*, to beg ; cf. Tshuana
　　kōna, to bow down, to bend ; Herero *hona*, to stoop low, to
　　crouch, creep ;
vkan (variation of *vkona*), to ask, beseech ;
vhan (allied to *vkona* and *vkan*), to creep, shrink ;
qganu (to go up, over, or through, the *a* being a substitute for an
　　original *u*), to cross a river ; Herero *konda ;*
qganu, prep. through ;
qkâu (contracted of *QGANU*, Bantu *konda, kondo*, primitive form
　　KU-TU = KU-N-TU, to go over or through), to ford a river,
　　cross over ;
qkau (for *QKANU*, to go up, over, through, go through with a
　　knife), to cut (through) ; Herero *konda, kondo ;* cf. Eng. *cut*,
　　nasalised *sund-er ; qkau-qa*, to cut asunder ;
qkau-s (*QKANU-S*), circumcision ;
vhanu-vhanu (go up, over, through, cut through, decide), administer
　　justice ;
vhanu, straight, right, just ;
vhanu-p, justice, rectitude ;
qanu-qanu (to go or run up, over, overflow, wash clean), to purify,

make holy ; cf. Herero *kona, kono* (*KUNDU*, to run up or over, as water), to flow over, to make clean, wipe ;
qanu, pure, clean, holy ;
qanu-p, purity, holiness.

Now all these words, so different in form and meaning, can, with the aid and guidance of the vowel-laws, be recognised as near akin to each other, as branches of the same root and stem, namely—

KUNDU

nasalised form of *KU-TU*, which, in various modified forms, means—

1. To go up, to rise, to run over, be full, overflow, wash clean, &c.
2. To go from above, down, to come down, to crouch, creep, beg, &c.
3. To go over or through, ford a river, go through with a sharp instrument, cut, sunder, separate, decide, &c.

In some of the above Nama words the radical vowel *u* has changed into *a ;* in others the first consonant has been encumbered with the click element (*c* = dental, *x* = lateral, *q* = cerebral, and *v* = palatal click) and the nasal *n* (remnant of *nd*) has disappeared—quite in keeping with the tendency in Hottentot to grind the root-words down to monosyllables—still all of them have retained so much of the original family likeness that they betray their close relationship to each other.

In the Aryan languages the consonantal skeleton of roots is more perfect, and the primitive radical vowel has been more gently dealt with, so that, as a rule, if lost in one, it has been preserved in another idiom. But in which? Here lies the difficulty. Comparative philologists are often not a little puzzled at the variety of vowel-sound in many a group of Aryan root-words, not to speak of the vowel-changes in moods and tenses. They are at a loss as to *which form ought to be placed at the head as the nearest approach to the original.* Now, in endeavouring to settle questions of this kind, the study of Bantu is indispensable : it will render material aid to the student, and in many perplexing cases point out to him the way to arrive at a satisfactory result. The English verb *to stand*, for example, sounds in O. Eng. *stonde*, A.-Sax. *stondan, standan*, Goth. *standan*, O. Fries. *stonda*, Dutch *staan*, Ger. *stehen*, Skr. *stâ*. Now which of these is the most perfect and approximately primitive form? Again, the verb *to bind* is in Sax. and O. Ger. *bindan*, Dutch *binden*, pret. *bond*, Ger. *binden*, pret. *band*, Skr. *bandh*. Which of these forms is the most original? If the student will take the trouble of examining Herero and kindred idioms in African Bantu and Polynesian, he will find sufficient reason to decide, in the former case, for the O. English *stonde* or O. Friesian *stonda*, and, in the latter, for Sanskrit *bandh*. For a comparison with Bantu and Polynesian leads to the discovery of *tundu* or *tutu* (*TU-TU*, nasalised *TU-N-DU*) as the primitive form of *s-tand* (*stonda*); Herero TUNDA, indicative *tundu*, "aufrecht stehen," *tund-ama*, to stretch *up*, be raised, elevated, stand high, &c.; Fijian *tu* (probably abbreviated from *tutu*), to stand, *ai-tutu*, a stand or place to stand on or in, allied to *donu*, Tongan *tonu* (*TONDU*), straight, right, correct; whilst the full original form of *to bind* has been preserved in Herero PANDA (*pand-eka*, to make go *together*, to bind; *oma-pando*, fetters), nasalised form of *pata*, to go or cause to go close *together*, to shut, close; Zulu *pata* (in several forms), to move, to draw *together*, to clasp, to shut close together, as an iron trap, to get close upon, engage in close fight, "handgemein werden," hence to touch, handle, pat; allied to Tongan *fatu* (in which the second *a* has changed to *u*), to tie, as rafters of a house, to make go together, to fold, *fatui*, to fold up, *mata-fatu*, hard, not easily made to cry, from *ma-ta*, eyes, and *fatu*, shut, literally eye-shut or eye-bound.

The following scheme is intended to represent the three principal powers of the primary vowels, the source of the various secondary meanings as stated before:—

a = on the ground, horizontal;
i = in, within (the body, earth, place, water, &c.);
u = above the ground, high, in the air, vertical.

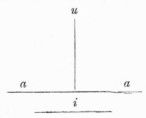

The Vowel-Laws Proved.—I shall now endeavour to illustrate and exemplify the laws that have been stated, and for that purpose invite attention to a few groups of Herero root-words. For brevity's sake, and in order to present a clearer view of the several groups, I shall, as a rule, give the verbs only in their simple form.

KAKA, TYIKA (KIKA), KUKA.

kaka (= to go or run on the surface of the earth, to beat a road, make hard, or go together, congeal, shrink), be hard, dry, get hard, get a crust;

tyika (= to go out of the straight line), incline to one side, stand oblique, be aslant;

xeka (= to go out of the straight line, out of its proper place), to be or go out of joint, to get loose (as a waggon), to relax (Zulu);

kuka (= to go or run up), to start, as for a journey, to travel; to overflow, sweep away, as a stream of water, clear off (Zulu (*kuk-ula*); swell, expand, swell with passion, pride, &c. (Zulu *kuku-mala*); to appear above the surface (Tshuana *kuku-nya*), to rise above the horizon, used of clouds (Tshuana *kuku-mologa*),

koka (= to run or go up, over, and the opposite, to move downward, bend, curve; to go ahead, in front, before, &c.), to rise up or swell out, as food boiling (Tshuana *koko-moga*); to run over, or make run over, fill, satisfy, pay, render what is due (Zulu); to go before, to lead (Xosa), hence Zulu *u-koko*, ancestor, progenitor, grandfather; to go before something, drag it over the ground (Herero *koka*, *koko-zora*, Tshuana *koko-tha*); move from above, downward, bend, curve, stoop, &c. (Zulu *koko-ba*, crouch or stoop in walking; *koko-beza*, subdue, put down; *ama-koko-ma*, stoop in the back; Herero *-koko*, curved, crooked; *koko-vara*, to be curved, crooked).— Modifications of the above are:—

kaha (= to run on the ground, harden the ground by running over it, or, to run together, congeal, become hard), to be hard, dry, firm, solid (*-kahe*);

haka (= run on the ground, run on, run fast), *haka-hana*, make haste, *oru-haka*, rashness;

hiha (= run out of the straight line, move to and fro, from one side to the other), be moved (with pain, pity), feel pain, feel pity (*hih-ama*), be moved with kindness towards others, be kind and considerate, be anxious to provide for the wants of others (*hiha*) ;

huka (= run up, rise), rise, get up, go away (Makonde), hence Herero *omu-huka*, morning, properly the rising fire or light ;

huha (= run downward, be bowed down, be bent, curved, round, go round), to bewitch, properly bind round, fetter ; *e-huha*, loop, tie ; *otyi-huha*, state of being bewitched, properly state of being bound, fettered ;

hoka (= run downward, go down, bow down, bend, curve, be round, and go round), put round, fence in, protect, as plants by a hedge, thatch a house (*hok-era*).

Nasalised forms of this group are :—

KANGA, TYINGA (KINGA), KUNGA.

kanga (= to run on the ground, to beat a road, make hard, or run together, congeal), to be hard, dry, or to make hard, dry ;

tyenga (= to run out of the straight line, or to run from within, out), to upset, as a pot containing food (*tyeng-ura*), to throw out ;

xenga-xenga (= to run or go out of the straight line, to move to and fro), to move from one side to the other, be shaky, loose (Zulu) ;

kunga (= to run up), to throw up, from the stomach, vomit ; to run over, as liquids ;

kunga (= to run downward, bend, curve, go or be round), to bind round, as a string of beads round the arm, or to put a rope round the neck of an animal, tie up an animal (Zulu) ;

konga (= to go over or through, to go before, hence also to follow), to go through with a sharp instrument, to sever ; to follow, lit. be fronted, run or go after something in front (*kong-orera*).

TATA, TITA, TUTA.

tata (= to stretch on the surface of the earth), to throw flat on the ground ;

tita (= to sink into), Konde *titi-ma*, sink into ; Zulu *titi-bala*, be

wet thoroughly, soaked, confounded, helpless (be as a drown-
ing one); *titi-nya*, to sound, as the depth of a river or a
person's meaning or purpose;

teta (= to put in or between, as the teeth or a knife, to divide), bite,
chew, crack, sever, crop;

tiza (= to turn out of the straight line, to place oblique), to lean
against, to prop, support;

tuta (= to reach up, to pile up), to carry and throw things together
in a heap, make a heap;

tuta and *tota* (= to go through, or to go round, as in making or
widening a hole), to hollow or be hollow (*-tutu*, *-toto*).—
Closely allied are :—

tara (= to stretch on the ground, stretch horizontally), to stretch,
extend (*tara-vara*);

tira (= to turn out of the straight line, turn aside), to fear; Tshuana
tila, to avoid, get out of the way of anything likely to harm;

tera (= to turn out of the straight line, from one side to the other),
to stagger (*tera-tera*);

tura (= to stretch upward, lift up), lift up anything (*tur-ika*); Zulu
tula in *u-tuli* (*uiu-tuli*), dust, disturbance, lit. rising; opposite
sense: *tula* (be put down, be subdued), be silent, mute, quiet,
calm, peaceful, be settled as water;

tura (= to stretch upward, lift up, as the fist or an instrument for
striking, crushing), to strike hard, pound, crush, as a bone;

tora or *toora* (= to stretch upward, lift up), lift up from the ground,
take up; Zulu *tola*, pick up, take up, &c.

Nasalised forms :—

TANDA, TINDA, TUNDA.

tanda (= to stretch, reach horizontally), to aim at, fix the eye as in
taking aim, have the eye on, hence to intend, devise mischief,
threaten (in Zulu to love); *tanda-vara*, to stretch, extend,
spread;

tinda (= to put between, to intervene), to resist, refuse (Zulu *tinta*,
to intercept, stop);

tenda (= to put between, as a sharp instrument, to divide), to cut;

tunda (= to stretch up, reach high), to rise, climb, be erect, high;

tonda (= to lift up, as a stick for beating, allied to the contracted form *tona*, to beat), to stamp, as with a pestle, to pound, to hate; (identical with Zulu *zonda*, to hate, abhor; have a fixed pain).

PAPA, PIPA, PUPA.

papa (= to squeeze close, together, as the fingers, wings, &c.), to be firm, solid, compact;

papa (= to spread out the wings, spread the wings on or near the ground), flap the wings, flutter (Zulu);

pepa (= to fly out of the straight course), start aside, avoid (Kafir);

pepa (= to blow into, or to blow out of the mouth), to make fire, blow up a fire;

pupa (= to blow or fly upward), to be light, easy (*-pupu*), to float.— Near akin are :—

vava or *papa* (= to spread, as wings, or a skin on the ground), to spread on the ground and fasten with pegs, as a hide to dry (*vav-era*, *pap-era*); *otyi-vava*, a wing;

viva (= to move out of the straight line, move to and fro, from one side to the other), to fan, wag, practise fencing, &c.; *viv-iza*, to whet, sharpen (from the motion), get ready for a fight (applied to a bull);

boba (= to quickly move downward), to stoop in order to hide, hide oneself behind something; *bob-ela*, to stoop forward, to subside, as a swelling (Tshuana);

bopa (= to quickly move downward, bow down, stoop, bend, curve, go round), bind round, fasten round the waist, as a belt, gird, wind a bandage round a wound, &c. (Zulu).

Nasalised forms :—

PAMBA, PIMBA, PUMBA.

pamba (= to move, squeeze close together), to plait, properly put things close together;

pimba (= to move out and step in, as in changing places or taking turns; to make room for another, or step into the place of another), to exchange, barter, requite, retaliate;

pumba (= to fly or rise quickly upward, or cause to move upward, to ease, remove a burden, as the superfluous branches of trees, make light), to prune, to lop; to take off the point, to blunt.

Meaning of the Vowels in the Herero Prefixes.—On this topic I can only give a few hints here. A fuller statement of my views on the original signification of the Bantu pronominal forms the student will find in Chapters VIII. and X., and in the Introduction to my English-Herero Dictionary. The Roman numbers here and elsewhere belong to Bleek's arrangement of the prefixes, based on Herero, as being of all Bantu idioms as yet discovered in South and Central Africa " the richest in classes of nouns." The reasons of my partially departing from Bleek's classification I have intimated in the aforesaid dictionary (p. xxviii.) As to the primitive forms in italic capitals, they will be explained in subsequent chapters.

*o*mu- (*KU-MU*) I ;—plur. *o*va- (*KHA*) II.

The vowel *u* in *o*mu- means *up*, upright, erect, this being the posture of man (*o*mu-*ndu*, Zulu *u*mu-*ntu*).

Originally the prefix *o*u-, *o*(**v**)u-, Zulu *u*-bu- (*KHU*) XIV. = men absolute, corresponded to *o*mu- as legitimate plural, but on assuming its present abstract meaning, as in *o*u-*ndu*, humanity (orig. men), *o*va-, Zulu *a*ba- (*KHA*) came into use. *A* in the plural prefix *o*va- means (men) in general, or spread over the earth, (men) abroad.

*o*n-, *o*m- (*KI-MI*) IX. ;—plur. *o*zo-*n*-, *o*-zo-*m*- (*KHA-KIMI*) X.

The fact that the prefix *o*n- (*o*in-, *i*n-), which is *the* prefix for names of animals, and its corresponding pronoun should appear, in all Bantu languages, with *i* as the radical vowel, has always been a puzzle to me, until quite recently the true cause has, I think, become clear to my mind. The vowel *i* in *i*n- IX. (animal, &c.) stands to *o*mu- (man) in somewhat the same relation as, *e.g.*, the Herero verb *yera* (*YIRA*) to *yura* (see Chapter VII.). Both verbs mean " to raise," but there is this primary difference : *yera* literally means to *out*lift, "*heraus*heben," while the original signification of *yura* is to *up*lift, "aufheben." So the prefix *o*mu- signifies a going-*up*, that is, a grown-*up*, upright, erect-moving being, man, but *o*n- (*i*n-), in virtue of the vowel *i*, a grown-*out*, *i.e.*, full-grown living thing; hence also Bantu *HI* (orig. animal-) father, and *NI* (orig. animal-) mother, the vowel *i* signifying here "out," and answering exactly to the German " *aus*gewachsen sein," full-grown, in distinction from young, immature, which originally was represented by the (now diminutive) prefix *o***ka-** ; the vowel *a* meaning in general (a living thing moving) *on the earth ;* hence *o*ma-*paha* (*KA-MA-paha*), a couple of *children,* twins (singular *KA,* at present **e-**) ; but *o*mu-*ndu* (*KU-MU-ndu*), the grown-up, upright pair (full-grown, complete *man,* orig. man and woman, father and mother, husband and wife), and *o*n-*gombe* (*KI-MI-kombe*), the grown-*out, i.e.,* full-grown ("aus-gewachsenes") pair of cattle, orig. ox *and* cow, at present ox *or* cow :—

KA = living thing generally *on the earth,* hence also child, young
     animal, living member of the body, &c.

KU = raised, grown-*up, upright* ("*auf*gewach sener") living one (man, father), and whatever resembles the erect human body.	*KI* = grown-*out, ex*panded, full-grown ("*aus*gewachsenes"), living thing (animal, father), and any object resembling an animal.

The vowel *a* in the plural *o***zo-***n-* (*KHA-KIMI*), corresponding pronoun *ze, za,* signifies on the earth, abroad, or in general :—*KI* = full-grown animal ; *KI-MI* = full-grown animal-pair ; *KHA-KIMI* = number of living things in general, or spread over the earth.

     *o*mu- (*FU-MU*) III. ;—plur. *o*mi- (*PI-MI*) IV.

U in *o*mu- means obviously *up* in the air, as the outstretched wings of a flying bird, the waving branches of trees ; hence the application of this prefix for waving things generally and whatever resembles them, as the branch-like finger-rows, the wing-like eyelids, the flapping lips, the waving river, &c.

     The plural *o*mi- is possibly just a phonetic variation (umlaut) of *o*mu-.

     e- (*TI*) and **e**- (*KA*) V. ;—plur. *o*ma- (*KA-MA*) VI.

The vowel *i* in e(**ri**-), Zulu *i*li-, prefix for names of *dead* things, means *in,* as the dead teeth (*e-yo*) *in* the mouth, the bones (*e-tupa*) *in* the body, the stones (*e-ue*) and metals *in* the earth. With the above *e*(**ri**-) V., another prefix, **e**- (*KE, KA*), identical with *o*ka- XIII., has coalesced, with the vowel-meaning *on the earth,*

KA signifying originally, as we stated just now, living thing on the earth, hence living thing generally, as e-*paha*, one of a twin-pair, e-*kono*, one of the living arms, &c. It is to this latter e- (*KA*) that

o*ma*- (*KA-MA*), originally a form of the sexal dual, now corresponds as plural. The original plural of e(ri-), which must have been something like *TI* (*THI*), has been supplanted by o*ma*-.

o*ru*- (*TU*) XI. ;—plur. o*tu*- (*THU*) XII.

U signifies here *up*, rising upward, high ; hence the nouns of this class embrace high, long and lengthened, thin objects.

*O*tu- is the original legitimate plural of o*ru*-.

o*tyi*- (*KI*) VII. ; plur. o*vi*- (*KHI*) VIII.

*O*tyi- (Kongo ki-, Zulu si-) is properly the singular of the sexual dual form o*n*- (o-*in*-, *in*-, *KI-MI*), which see. Originally *KI* signified full-grown animal (" *aus*gewachsenes thier "), but at present it is a neuter prefix with the general meaning " thing."

*O*vi- is its primitive natural plural.

o*ka*- (*KA*) XIII. ;—plur. o*u*- (*KHU*) XIV.

The meaning of the vowel *a* here is *on the earth*. *O*ka-, at present diminutive in Herero and other idioms, must, as we said before, have meant originally living thing in general, child, young animal (hence diminutive), in distinction from *KU* (grown up, great, or erect living one) and *KI* (big, " *aus*gewachsenes," full-grown living thing).

The plural o*u*- (*KHU*), in Angola tu (*THU* = *KHU*), instead of o*va*- (*KHA*) or o*zo*- (*THA* = *KHA*), is an irregularity which probably arose from the disturbance caused by the substitution of o*va*- (*KHA*) II. for the original plural (now abstract) prefix o*u*- (*KHU*).

o*u*- (*PU*) XIV. ;—plur. o*ma-u*- VI.

The vowel *u* of the singular prefix o*u*- has the same meaning as *u* in o*mu*- (*PU-MU*) III., namely, *up* in the air, high, as the boughs of trees. Thus o*u*- in o*u-ta*, bow, is properly the singular of the sexual dual o*mu*- in o-*mu-ti*, tree ; its original meaning is *one* of the wings or branches of a tree, a bough, a bough for shooting (o*u-ta*), *i.e.*, a bow.

C

The plural *o*ma-*u-ta* means literally *both* bows, that is, more than one, a number.

*o*ku- (*KU*) XV. ;—plur. *o*ma- or *o*ma-*ku*- VI.

U in *o*ku- is the same as *u* in *o*mu- (*KU-MU*) I.   Its force is *up*, *upright*, *erect* as man, pointed, *high*, hence also distant : *o*ku-*tui*, ear (originally not any ear, but the pricked-up, pointed ear, as of a horse or an ass, hence also) *o*ku-*iya*, thorn (one of a couple of those long straight thorns which resemble the pricked-up ears of an animal) ; *o*ku-*oko*, the perpendicular man-like living member, front-leg of an animal, hence also arm, and *o*ku-*rama*, originally hind-leg of an animal, at present leg in general ; *o*ku-*ti*, field, woodland, probably tree with a *head* like the erect high head of man, or head high up in the air, bushy head of trees, bush, forest, country, to which latter noun the infinitive *o*ku- (= motion *to* a place or *to* an object at some distance) probably refers.

The legitimate primitive plural of *o*ku- is *o*u- (*KHU*) XIV., but as this form has been appropriated as an abstract and as plural of *o*ka-, and as, moreover, the corresponding dual *o*mu- (*KU-MU*) has been set apart for *man* (*o*mu-*ndu*), the *a*-form of the latter prefix, *o*ma- (*KA-MA*), is now in use as plural (properly dual) of *o*ku- : *o*ku-*tui*, ear, *o*ma-*tui*, ears, properly couple of ears ; *o*ku-*iya*, thorn, *o*ma-*ku-iya*, thorns, properly a couple of pointed ear-like things. Irregularities like the above, in the correspondence between singular and plural, date from the remote period when the original powers of the vowels ceased to be known.

The local prefixes *o*po-, *o*ko-, and *o*mo- are briefly treated in Chapter V.

Reasons for the Vowel-Laws.—But how, it remains still to be examined, came the vowel *a* to mean on the ground, horizontal ; the vowel *i* inward, within ; and the vowel *u* upward, on high ?

As we can still trace the original meaning of the primitive consonants *k*, *t*, and *p* in both pronoun (or primitive noun) and verb, such a question ought not to be regarded as presumptuous.   We know for certain that *k* originally meant to breathe, to live, to run, to walk, *t* to be dead, to lie, stretch, and *p* to blow, to wave, to fly. Now, it is evident that these letters, when first uttered by primeval man, were not pronounced vowelless as *k'*, *t'*, *p'* ; they must have come forth, as it were, twin-born, with a vowel joined to them. And if we further inquire which were the twin-sisters of *k*, *t*, *p* respectively, we shall not hesitate to admit that the organs of speech point to *a* as the natural companion of the guttural *k*; to *i* as most intimately connected with the dental *t*, and to *u* as being nearest akin to the labial *p*. These three twin-born primary articulate sounds are entirely independent of each other. "Man kann im allgemeinen sagen : die articulation des *k* beginnt da, wo die für das *t* aufhört, und umgekehrt" (Brücke). *Ka* naturally bursts forth from the throat (and palate), and does not require the aid either of the teeth or lips; *ti* as easily takes its origin from contact of the tongue with the teeth, independent of the throat and lips; and as to *pu*, it can be produced by the mere motion of the lips (as in blowing), without receiving help from either teeth, throat, or palate. In short, a trial with each of the three organs of speech (throat and palate, teeth, lips) *separately* will call forth from the throat (and palate) the sound *ka*, from the teeth (and tongue) *ti*, and from the lips *pu*.

Now, as running, walking (*ka*, *a*) is done *on the ground*; blowing, waving, flying (*pu*, *u*) is observed *in the air, on high*; and as the *dead* teeth and bones are *within* the mouth and body, it is perfectly intelligible that Adam may have been led to apply the vowel-sound *a* to living things and motions *on the ground*, *u* to waving objects and motions *in the air overhead*, and *i* to *dead* things, and at the same time to any motions and conditions that are *within* or *hidden*, like the rows of teeth *in* the mouth, the bones *in* the body, and the stones and metals *in* the earth.

CHAPTER IV.

THE VOWEL-METHOD IN UNIVERSAL ETYMOLOGY.

THE primeval vowel-laws, whose operation in Herero is too plain to admit of doubt, furnish us, as I have shown in former papers, with a new method of word-comparison—a method which, unshackled by the different grammatical superstructures, goes in a direct way to the body of language, and which therefore may be called the *direct method* of word-comparison, or also, as it springs from a knowledge of the laws of the vowels, the *vowel-method*. Its outlines are as follows :—

1. No true root-word stands isolated in language; it is a member of a family, in close relationship to a more or less numerous group; and each group of roots is, whatever individual difference there be, pervaded by one leading idea. We have thus, in universal etymology, to treat a root-word as in affinity and relation to the whole group. We do not compare isolated words in the several families of speech; we confront genera with genera, species with species.

2. The classification of root-words into genera and species is effected by the primary consonants K, T, P (with an additional primitive M in the pronominal roots), and the primeval vowel-sounds A, I, U. In a genus we have root-words with the vowels *a, i, u,* and kindred shades of sound, but a species comprises only roots of one primary vowel and its kindred sounds. Thus in Herero the genus PaTa would comprise roots as the following :—*pata, paza, vaza; pita, piza, vira, vera; puta, puza, pura;* whereas a species would be confined to *pata, paza,* &c., a second species to *pita, pitha, vera,* &c., and a third to *puta, puza, pora,* &c. ; future researches are sure to suggest subdivisions, but so much may be established even now as fundamental, that it is the consonants which mark off the genera, and the

vowels the species (and sub-species); or, in other words, motion gives the genus; direction varies it into species; thus :—

GENUS.	Species.
K-T = go .	*kata*, go on the ground, go together, &c. *hita* (*KITI*), go in, enter, &c. *kuta* (*KUTU*), go up, over, &c.

3. Now each genus is pervaded by one leading idea, generally to go, to move, to run, to stretch, to reach, to wave, and the like, the vowels modifying the sense, as has been stated before, producing, as a rule, seemingly *opposite* by-meanings, as together and scattered, upward and downward, in and out; and *wherever we find this phenomenon in the several families of speech (however imperfectly the roots may have been preserved), there we discover true relationship and original unity.* The very fact, for example, that the root *PATA* means in Herero (*pata*) to shut, in Hebrew (*patah*) to open or expand, and in Latin to be open, free, expanded (*pateo*), warrants our identifying these words; for the root *PATA* means both to go or run together, to shut, and the opposite, to go asunder, to spread, to expand.

The genus K*a*T*a* will serve as an illustration and specimen of universal etymology, in accordance with the rules of the vowel-method.

In Bantu the root *kata* has the meaning to fold, to glue together, to cleave together, stick to, be attached to, &c. In Fijian we have " *kata, a.,* close together, touching, as boards on a floor, so as to leave no crevice; *va-kata, a.,* shut, close " (Hazlewood's " Fijian Dictionary "). Now as the Polynesian languages stand in a sisterly relationship to African Bantu, based on the principle of grammatic identity, I expect to find it so, and there is no doubt in my mind concerning the identity of the Bantu and Polynesian *kata*. It is different when I turn to other families of speech. The Bantu-Polynesian *kata*, to cleave together, to be close together, reminds me of the Aryan root *KAT*- in Lat. *catena*, Germ. *kette*, Dutch *keten*, *chain;* and as *k* and *g* are closely allied, also the root *GAT*- (*gad-, gath-,* in Germ. *gatte*, Dutch *gade*, spouse, *gader, gaderen,* Engl. *gather*) occurs to me. Now the question arises, Is the

Aryan root *KAT-* (*gat-*, *gath-*, *gad-*) identical with the Bantu-Polynesian *kata?* Without some law to guide me, the answer to this question must be mere guesswork. But here the vowel-method steps in and regulates the inquiry, and I reason thus : *Kata* in Bantu-Polynesian is only a member of a genus of root-words whose leading idea is to *go*. *Kata* is a root of that species which, in virtue of the vowel *a*, means to go together, &c., closely allied to other species, as *kita* (*hita, shita*) and *kuta* (*kota*), which respectively mean to go in, and from within, out, to go over and through, &c. Now if I discover in the Aryan family the very same phenomenon ; if I find forms like *KATA* (*cat-*, *ket-*, *gat-*, *gath-*) with the primary meaning to go *together*, and parallel *i*-forms, *KITI* (*hid-*, *shid-*, *shit*), with the seemingly opposite meanings to go *in* and to go *out ;* as also parallel *u*-forms, *KUTU*, *KOTO*, denoting primarily to go *up*, over, through, and from above, *down :* then I have evidence as strong as can be expected in philology that *kata* in Bantu-Polynesian and *kat-* (*ket-*, *cat-*, *gat-*, *gad-*) in Aryan are identical.

Genus KaTa.

First Species.

KATA = to go on the ground, to go together.

Bantu : *kata* (to go together, hence) to stick to, cleave to, attach to, as *e.g.* thorny grass to clothes, to smear, plaster, paste on, make to stick to (Zulu) ; from this *in-kata* (Zulu), *on-gata* (Herero), *n-gata* (Konde), coil, ring or knot of grass, a pad ; *n-gata* (Tshuana), bound-up package, bundle ; *omu-kato* (Herero), trunk of an elephant, lit. the coiling-up, rolling-up lips or skin ; *on-gata-oko* (Herero), slowness, unsteadiness in one's work, lit. arm-coil, close folding of the arms ; *kata* (Herero), to shrink together, of plants, dry up, wither, reduplicated *kakatera*, *KA(TA)KATAIRA*, to stick to, cleave to ; allied to *hata*, reflex. *rihata* (Herero), to coil oneself up, as in sitting stoopingly on the ground, with crossed legs ; allied to *sata* (Zulu), draw together, embrace, have connection with a woman, *sat(anisa)*, fasten on one thing to another, as the blade of an assegai to the haft.

A strengthened form of *kata* is *kanda* (Herero), to run together, to congeal. The meaning *on the ground* we have in *yata* (Herero), to go on the ground, to tread, step, nasalised or strengthened *yanda*, "fest auftreten," walk with firm steps, run, run fast, far, out of sight, cease, end.

Polynesian : *kata* (Fijian), close together, touching, as boards on a floor, so as to leave no crevice.

Aryan : *kette* (Germ.), *keten* (Dutch), *catena* (Lat.) ; *gadde* (Icel.), to press together; *gador* (A.-Sax.), *gather* (Engl.), *gader*, *gaderen* (Dutch) ; *gatte* (Germ.), *gade* (Dutch), spouse, consort, mate—words which appear to be radically identical with Bantu-Polynesian *kata*. With Herero *yanda* or *anda*, to cease, end, the Sanskr. *anta*, Goth. *andeis*, Engl. *end* may be compared.

Second Species.

KITI = to go in, between, to go out.

Bantu : *hita* (Herero), to go in, to go between; allied to *tyinda* (*kinda*), to go from within or out, to leave a place, as nomads, remove, and to *hinda*, to cause to go out, to send (Herero) ; *tyera* (Herero), to go between, intercept, waylay, aim at one, try to seduce, allied to *tyiza* (Herero), perceive, discern, orig. go between.

Polynesian : *hili* in *faka-hili-hili* (Tongan), to intercept, turn into another route ; *hele* in *faka-ma-hele*, to cut in two, *helu*, scissors, comb ; *helu-helu*, to comb, properly make a path, divide the hair ; *kilā* (Fijian), to know, understand, regard, literally go between, discern.

Aryan : *shide* (O. Engl.), *skid* (Icel.), splinter ; *scidan* (A.-Sax.), to cleave, split, divide ; *scheiden* (Germ. and Dutch), to go between, separate, part ; *scheitel* (Germ.), *schedel* (Dutch), crown of the head, probably from the dividing of the hair ; *scirian, scerian* (A.-Sax.), to go between, to divide, to part among two or more, allied to *shear, share ;* the seemingly opposite meaning from within, from between or out, being found in the nasalised or strengthened form *send*, Icel. *senda*, to go or cause to go out.

Third Species.

Kutu = to go up, over, through, down.

Bantu : *kuta* (Herero), be filled with food, properly be running over ; *suta* (Zulu), eat or drink to one's satisfaction, be full, sated ; *suta* (Herero), pay one's debts, also moral debts, satisfy, atone, lit. make run over, fill up ; opposite meaning : *kota* = *kora* (Herero), to go downward, bow down, bend down, be crooked, curved, bent ; nasalised or strengthened form *kunda* (Herero), to go over, run over, be full (of numbers) ; allied to *konda*, to go over or through, also to go through with a sharp instrument, to cut through, to saw.

Polynesian : *koro-koro* (Fijian), heaps, as of sandbanks (lit. a running up or high, a great quantity, a mass, a meaning which *-koro* also has in Herero) ; *koro-(nimuna)*, the prominent parts of the buttock on each side of the backbone ; *gutu-va* (Fijian), to cut off (go over, through) ; *faka-goto* (Tongan), to go down, sink, press under water.

Aryan : *sat* (in which the original *u* has given place to *a*), A.-Sax. *sad*, sated, Germ. *satt*, Dutch *zat*, Lat. *satis*, enough (full, running over) ; *kuta*, to cut with a knife, *kuti*, a small knife (Icel.) ; *kotta* (O. Swed.) = Engl. *cut*, allied to *sunder*, Germ. *sondern*, to go or cut through. The opposite meaning, to go down, be bowed down, bent, we have in such words as *crook* (*KUR = KUT*), Icel. *crôkr*, Swed. *krok*, a curve ; cf. *cur* in Lat. *curvus*, bent, arched.

The above words form, of course, only a small part of the wide-spread ramifications, both in Bantu and Aryan, of the genus KaTa, but they will answer our present purpose, and be helpful, in some measure, in showing the scope and working of the vowel-method.

CHAPTER V.

NOTES ON THE PRIMITIVE BANTU PREPOSITIONS AND ADVERBS.

1. THE high antiquity of the prepositions and adverbs of space, *PA* (= at, by, near), *MU* (= in, within, present), and *KU* (= to, above, on, off, at a distance, &c.), is evident from the fact that they occur in a more or less perfect form in all Bantu idioms.

2. The reason why there are three is, *because they have stepped into the place of the three primary vowels, A, I, U.* When the reign of the latter ceased and their laws became obsolete, it was found necessary to choose other signs for expressing those relations of space which had been indicated before by vowel-sounds.

3. *PA* became the successor of *a*, *MU* of *i*, and *KU* of *u*. In the forms *PA* and *KU* the original vowel-meaning is obvious (*a* = at or near the ground, not high in the air; *u* = upward, above, on the top, and from above, down, &c.), but in *MU* it is exclusively the consonant *m* to which the idea in, within (orig. mother, womb, inner and present place), attaches; in other words, *m* as preposition, adverb, or particle means always in, present, whether it be pronounced with *u* (*MU*), *a* (*MA*), or *i* (*MI*).

4. The preposition (and adverb) *PA* is radically identical with the Herero prefix *opo-* (*PA*) in *opo-na* XVI. = a place near, at hand, allied to the prefix *ou-* (sing., prim. r. *PU*), as in *ou-ta* (*PU-ta*), bow, properly bough, *one* of the wing-like branches of an *omu-ti* (*PU-MU-ti*), tree. *PA*, as a primitive noun, probably signified originally the human hand and foot, both being looked upon, as they are in Bantu to this very day, as wing-like objects, on account of the branch-resembling fingers and toes, which, therefore, in Herero are still denoted by one and the same name, *omu-nue* (*PU-MU-nue*) = the wing-like member, *PU-MU* signifying originally a pair of wings (as

of a bird, flying *in the air*, or the wing-like branches of a tree, waving high *in the air*) : hence the *a*-form of *PU : PA* = wing or branch of the human body *on* or *near the ground* = hand (or foot) = at hand, at, near, close by.   The vowel *u* in the Herero preposition *pu*, and *o* in the adverb *po* are substitutes for an original *a*.

5. The primitive Bantu noun *PA* XVI. runs parallel with the verb *pa*, to give, properly make grasp (with the branch-like finger-row or hand), and with *pa* in Bantu *papa, vava* (fly near the ground, flutter, stretch or flap the wings, spread, as a skin on the ground, &c.), from which Herero e-*pa*, branch, and o*tyi-vava*, wing.

6. As, therefore, the Bantu monosyllable *PA* means *a.* (at) hand, near, close by, and *b.* to (cause to) grasp, give, it is probably identical with the Chinese " classifier " *pa*, which means " to seize, to grasp, or lift up with one hand, being applied to many things held in the hand by a handle when used," and also with our preposition and adverb *by*, A.-Sax. *be, bi* (near to, by, of, from), Goth. *bi*, Germ. *bei* = at hand, near, at, on, &c., originally the same as the prefix *be*- (A.-Sax. *be* and *bi*, Goth. *bi*, Germ. *be* and *bei*) in *be*fore, *be*cause, *be*ware.

7. The preposition *MU* is radically identical with the Herero prefix *o*mo- (*MU*) XVIII. in omo-*na*, cavern, grotto, house, inner or present place, the primitive noun *MU* signifying, as we said before, mother, womb = in, present.   It has also been stated already that in this preposition the notion *in* is transferred from the vowel *i* to the consonant *m*, which means *in, within, present*, even when pronounced with *u* (*MU*) or *a* (*MA*).   The Herero adv. and conj. *nu* (= now, and) is an offshoot of *mu* = in, present.   Compare our adv. and conj. *now*, Goth., Dutch, Dan., Swed. *nu*, O. Sax., O. Germ., and Icel. *nû* = at the present time.   The Bantu preposition *na* = present, near, with, and, &c., is a modification of *MA*, *a*-form of *MU*.

8. The preposition *KU* is radically identical with the Herero prefix *o*ko- (*KU*) in *o*ko-*na* XVII. = distant place (orig. head or high place, top-place, also bush, woodland, extent of country, &c., height and length or distance being the same thing in Bantu).   The primitive noun *KU* signifies the great, erect, or high living one, hence man; but in the primitive language it was also probably applied to the high living member of the body, the head, as we may infer from the Herero noun o*ku-ti* XV., field (wood, bush,

forest), land, country:—*ti* = wood: *o*mu-*ti* (*PU-MU-ti*), tree, properly *winged* or branching wood, tree, the branches being compared to a pair of wings; *o*ru-*ti*, a long stick, as a long whip-stick, properly a *horn*-tree, a piece of wood, long and thin, as a horn; *o*ku-*ti*, bush, forest, field, country, literally *head*-wood, *i.e.*, *high* and great wood, or tree with a *high* bushy *head* or crown, hence bush, forest, country, distant place. *KU* was, therefore, well fitted for expressing the notion " on the top, high," and also " long, distant, in front, &c." The *oku* of the infinitive is a secondary form, derived from the primitive *KU* as occurring in *o*ku-*ti*.

9. As the Bantu pronoun *ku* (thou, thee) is in Aryan *tu*, so is probably also in our preposition and directive *to* (Sax. and O. Fries. *to*, Goth. *du*, *tu*, Germ. *zu*) the dental a changed *k*. The Bantu *ku* is used in exactly the same way as our *to* : *ma vanga okuya ku ami* (Herero) = he-wants-to come-*to*-me; up *to* heaven, *k'eyuru* (*ku-eyuru*). That our *to* originally not only meant " motion toward, extent," but also " high, up, over, on," like the Herero *ko*, appears from the emphasised *too* (A.-Sax. *tô*, Germ. *zu*, as in *da-zu*, *zu gross*, *zugeben*), over, more than enough, in addition. The demonstrative *so* (coupled with *al* : *also*) too seems to be a modified form of *to*, and if so, it betrays the existence, at a very remote period, either of a monosyllabic noun *KU* (*TU*), or of a noun which had *KU* (*TU*) for a suffix or prefix (as in the Bantu xv. *KU* class), and to which noun *so* corresponded as a demonstrative pronoun.

10. The result thus of our inquiry into the nature and original meaning of the three principal Bantu prepositions is as follows :—

PA = wing, branch, or branch-like object *near the ground*, human wing or branch-like member, *i.e.*, hand (foot) = at hand, **by**, near, close by, not high up in the air, but on or near the surface of the earth, corresponding to the primary meaning of the vowel *a*.

MU = mother = womb, womb-like place, cavern, grotto, house = in (and out), inner or present place, present, no*w* (**nu**), corresponding to the primary meaning of the vowel *i*.

KU = the high living one = head = top, bush, height, length, distance, extent, motion **to** (and from), on high, on the top, in addition, **too** (tô), upon (and from upon), off, &c., corresponding to the primary meaning of the vowel *u*.

Accordingly, the three local Herero nouns to which the three primitive Bantu prepositions and adverbs correspond, appear to have the following primary meaning :—

*o***po**-*na* (*PA-na*), hand-place, *i.e.*, at hand place, a place which is near, close *by.*

*o***mo**-*na* (*MU-na*), mother- or womb-like place, inner place, hence also present place, *in* which one *now* is.

*o***ko**-*na* (*KU-na*), head- or top-place (high, hence also) distant place, *to* which one has to move.

For some further remarks on the nature of the Bantu prepositions, see § 32 in the Introduction to the author's English-Herero Dictionary.

CHAPTER VI.

ROOT-FORMATION: ITS BEGINNINGS AND SUCCESSIVE STAGES.

THE first utterances of man were monosyllabic, regulated by the simple laws we have stated in former chapters. They consisted of one consonant and one vowel, the former taking in all cases the precedence, as *ka, ti, pu.*

Now we may observe that such primitive monosyllables served in a double capacity, namely, as a name for a person or thing (noun, pronoun), and as a term for a motion, action, or condition (verb). The monosyllable *KA*, for instance, means the living, running, walking one, but also to move, to run, to go. *KA* embodies thus originally subject and predicate; it conveys the meaning of a whole sentence; noun and verb proceed from it in the following manner:—

KA = the runner runs.

ka = (the) runner.   *ka* = (is) running.

Here we have the *first* or **germinal** stage in root-formation. The first beginnings of language must have been something like the following:—

1. Throat.

KA = the breathing, living, running one, animal, moving spontaneously;
to breathe, live, move spontaneously; run, go, strike the ground, &c.

2. Teeth.

TI = the (inner) dead one, tooth, bone;
to be dead, motionless, die, lie, &c.

3. Lips.

PU = the blowing, waving one, wind, wing, branches and leaves of trees, waves of a lake, river, finger-rows, as resembling branches, &c. ;

to blow as the wind, move, wave high in the air, fly, be light, float, &c.

Sentences.

Germinal Stage—First Step.

KA = the living one runs; the fleshy one (arm, leg) is alive, moving;

TI = the dead one is motionless, hard, solid;

PU = the blowing one (wind) shakes the branches, makes them wave in the air, &c.

Second Step.

KA KA = the animal is running;

KA TI = the animal is dead;

KA PU = the animal (bird) flies ;

TI TI = the dead one (as the stem of a tree, plant) is dead, dry ;

TI KA = the dead one (stem) has life, sap ;

TI PU = the dead one (as stubble, husk) flies up;

PU PU = the waving one (wing, branch) is flying (waving) in the air ;

PU KA = the blowing one (wind) runs over (sweeps) the ground ;

PU TI = the waving one (branch, bough) is dead, dry (severed from the tree).

In the *second stage* we find the three primitive vowels applied to each primitive monosyllable. This we shall call the **monosyllabic** stage.

Examples.

a. Nouns.

KA = the breathing, living one, runner or walker on the ground; or the living, fleshy one generally;

KI = the full-grown (properly *out*grown, " ausgewachsene ") living one, as a full-grown animal;

KU = the erect-moving living one, man, and whatever resembles him ;

TI = the inner dead one, tooth (*in* the mouth, or *in* the jaw), bone (*in* the body);
TA = the dead one, or sleeping, lying one, prostrate on the ground, the stretching one;
TU = the rising dead one, the high or long dead one, the erect dead one;

PU = the blowing one, wind, air, lips, the waving one, branch, wing, &c.;
PA = the waving one (not high in the air, but) on or near the ground, the wing-like member of the human body, hand (with the branch-like finger-row) or foot (with the row of toes); hence also the grasping, leaping one;
PI = the inner, hidden, waving one, also the out-flying or out-springing one, &c.

b. Verbs.

KA = breathe, live, move voluntarily, as animals, or have animal life, as the living members of the human and animal body; to run, also to strike the ground, to strike, hew down, as a tree (Herero *ka*); run on the ground, run together. (See the law of vowel *a*);
KI = to go or run in, between, and from within, out, go out of the straight line, be oblique, turn aside, avoid, &c. (See the law of vowel *i*);
KU = to go or run up, and from above, down, run over, through, &c. (See the law of vowel *u*);

TI = to be motionless, dead;
TA = be like a dead one, stretch, lie, sleep on the ground;
TU = lie up, rise, stretch up, reach high.

PU = to blow, cause a waving motion high in the air, move, as on wings, upward, be light, floating, &c.
PA = to blow over the ground, to move quickly along the ground, as leaves driven by the wind; to flap with the wings; to move with the wing- or branch-like hand or fingers, to grasp; also to leap (fly, grasp) as a pouncing animal (on the ground, not high in the air).

PI = to blow in, as in sticks to make fire; to grasp from within, take out, jump out, &c.

Now comes the *third* or **juxtapositional** stage. Two monosyllabic roots are placed next to each other, one elucidating or determining the other, and thus becoming a proper medium of communicating thought. As, for example, *KA TA*. *KA* means simply to live, move spontaneously, and might therefore be employed for any movement of any living thing; so the root *TA* was added, which means to stretch, as the leg or foot in walking; *KA TA* = move-stretch (the legs, feet), hence to tread, step (Herero *yata*), step firmly, go fast, run (Herero *yanda*), &c.; *KA PA* = move-grasp, seize, catch (Tshuana *kapa;* other dialects, *kamba*).

After this, root-formation entered upon its *fourth* or **combinatory** stage, in which the two monosyllabic roots of the third stage were glued together, each losing its individual character, and both becoming one dissyllabic root-word, as *KA + TA* = move + stretch : *KATA* = tread, step, walk ; *KA + PA* = move + grasp : *KAPA* = catch ; *TA + PA* = stretch (as the paw) + grasp : *TAPA* = stretch the paw, as in taking something out of a hole (Herero *tapa*, to take honey from a hole), or put the paw on, lay firmly hold of, refuse (Herero *zapa*, Zulu *zaba*, refuse, properly fix the paw or foot, stand firm, be immovable).

Lastly, we have what may be called the **modificatory** stage. Here various forces may be observed to have been at work.

1. *Aspiration.*—Aspirated or strengthened consonants have, in verbal roots, transitive, causative, emphasising, and frequentative power. In Herero the aspirates (*kh, th,* and *ph*) have lost their original sound; nevertheless their former existence and functions in the verb can, to some extent, still be traced in their present substitutes *v, z,* &c.—(cf. Chapter VIII.). In pronominal roots—for already in the monosyllabic stage the process of aspiration was resorted to—the aspirated or strengthened consonants mean *many, much,* thus forming the plural; as, for example, *o*ru- (orig. *TU*), one high, rising, or long object : *o*tu- (orig. *THU*), a number of such objects, many; *o*tyi- (*KI*), one thing : *o*vi- (*KHI*), many things. See the primeval law of the plural in the next chapter.

2. *Softening* of a tenuis to a media or liquida, as—

tata, lay prostrate, throw down flat on the ground ;
DADA or *lala*, *rara*, lie down, sleep.

3. *Nasalisation.*—Also the mode of nasalising and thus strengthening a root is evidently very old and belongs to this stage. In Herero the nasalised tenuis becomes, without exception, a media : *k* becomes *ng*, *t nd*, and *p mb*. For instance :—

kaka, to be hard ;
kanga (*kang-ura*), to harden much, as bricks, earthen vessels, by fire.

yata, to step, tread ;
yanda, to tread, step firmly, run fast, run far, away, get out of sight, disappear, cease.

puta, go down to the ground, stumble ;
punda, move downward from a height, descend.

4. *Contraction.*—Now such nasalised or strengthened roots (as *yanda* from *yata*, *tonda* from *tota*, *kamba* from *kapa*) once being formed, they were afterwards contracted, in order to serve as signs for different shades of thought. Thus we have in Herero :—

kamba (*kamb-ura*), grasp, seize, catch ;
kama, press together, squeeze, squeeze out.

tonda, stamp, pound ;
tona, beat.

pamba, put close together, plait ;
pama, be compressed.

yanda, run fast, far ;
yana (run together, agree, confederate, join, form an alliance, hence) to affirm on oath, swear.

5. *Abbreviation.*—Abbreviation too is an important factor in root-formation. This is so well known that one specimen will suffice here as an illustration. Let us take the last root-word in the above row, *yana* = to swear, state on oath, properly to go together, agree,

D

&c., hence also to marry, as in the identical Zulu *gana* = to marry (of a female), be united to a husband; *um-gani* (= *um-gane* or *um-ngane*), companion, mate, friend.   Now, by aphæresis, the initial *g* (*y*) being dropped, the sign was formed for the reciprocal form of the verb, namely, *-ana* = together, each other :—

> *yumba*, to throw ;
> *yumb-ana*, to throw (darts, javelins) at *each other*, fight to- gether, make war.

The literal meaning of *-ana* being, like *gana*, *yana*, to *go together*.

6. *Lengthening the vowel*, or also *colouring the primary vowel*, as—

> *tura* (in *tur-ika*), to lift up ;
> *toora* (Zulu *tola*), to take up, carry away.

> *tiza*, to lean against, prop, support ;
> *teza*, to act against, stop, overtake, as stolen cattle, turn, check the progress of, follow a track, pursue.

7. *Transposition*, which mode, like that of *reduplication* (as in Herero *ra-ra*, sleep, *ta-ta*, throw down), must have commenced in the juxtapositional stage, but which was carried on throughout to the last stage, as Herero *tana* and *nata*, to throw down; *zapa* and *pa(nd)za*, to refuse.

Here the primitive root-formation stopped. The vowel-laws have, in the whole domain of roots, only power over monosyllables and dissyllables, that is, two monosyllables combined; in a word with three syllables, as, for example, Herero *kaseka* (move to a distance), one syllable is additional and inorganic (in the quoted instance the first syllable, *ka*).

As to the question what time language required to pass through the afore-mentioned stages, I am aware that some scholars assume periods of very long duration—a hundred thousand, or even many hundred thousands of years. But others take what would seem the wiser and safer course, and frankly confess, " We don't know; we can't tell." If we had no English history, philologists would probably be tempted to assign to the causes which moulded from a pure Teutonic idiom the English of to-day a period much longer than that which is historically authenticated. Why increase the number of miracles? If the human race is as old as many hundreds of thousands of years, it could only have been by a miracle that language was preserved in so primitive a state as we still find it in Herero. There is no reason why the first four stages of root-formation should not have been gone through in the first century after the creation of man, or, at any rate, during the lifetime of the first generation of mankind; to the last or modificatory stage a longer period may be assigned. This, however, is certain, that all the stages described were passed through before the several families of language separated. Even Chinese and kindred idioms passed through the combinatory and modificatory stages of root-formation, though grammatically retaining the primitive character of an isolating language; whilst others became agglutinative, of which some afterwards advanced to inflection. But the process of root-formation came to a close with the dissyllabic modificatory stage, no true root in any language exceeding two primitive syllables.

The possibility of tracing a dissyllabic root-word in Herero to its very first source through all the stages of root-formation will appear from the following table:—

The Successive Stages of Root-Formation traced in Herero.

1. Germinal	KA $\begin{cases} \text{= the living one} \\ \text{= live, move} \end{cases}$	TI $\begin{cases} \text{= the dead one.} \\ \text{= be dead.} \end{cases}$	
2. Monosyllabic	KA = to live, move, run	TA = to die ; stretch, reach.	
3. Juxtapositional	KA TA	= move, stretch (= go).	
Transposed	TA KA	= stretch, move (= go).	
Reduplicated	KA KA	= run, run.	
	TA TA	= stretch, stretch.	
4. Combinatory	KATA	= go together, join, &c.	
Transposed	TAKA	= go together, mix (Zulu).	
5. Modificatory	YATA	= move, stretch (the leg), tread.	
	YANDA, HANDA	= step firm, run fast.	
	YANA	= go together, covenant, swear.	
	-ANA	= together, each other.	

CHAPTER VII.

ON THE DEVELOPMENT OF THOUGHT IN AFRICAN BANTU.

In the preceding chapter we endeavoured to give the germs and first products of the intimate union of intuitive thought and language. We shall now proceed to make a few remarks on the subsequent development of thought, as still traceable in the Bantu family. The subject is, of course, too vast to admit of anything like an exhaustive treatment in a single chapter. We can offer only a few hints here, and shall, in the first place, bring under review such terms of thought in the Bantu mind as at the same time shall serve to clear up and set right some seeming discrepancies or irregularities in connection with the laws and principles set forth in these pages, more especially as it regards the primeval laws of the vowels. The student will meet, now and then, with a Bantu word whose radical vowel would seem to flatly contradict our statements concerning the inherent powers of the three primary vowels, *a, i, u;* but in most cases the difficulty will be satisfactorily removed by tracing the line of thought which led to the use of the word in question for describing an action or condition which, at first view, would seem to require a different vowel.

We begin with the Zulu verb *paka-ma*, to rise, to be elevated. The ending *-ma*, means *to be* (in a fixed state or condition). The root is *paka*, the radical vowel thus *a*. But how can the notion to rise up, to be elevated, be represented by *a*, which, according to our statement, means on the ground, horizontal, together? There is no reason to suppose that the *a* in *paka* is a changed *u*, as, for instance, the *a* in *tamba* (tame, soft, gentle), which clearly is a modification of *tumba* (bring down, subdue, take or carry away captive). A comparison of Zulu *paka* with Herero *paka* will lead us on the right track, and clear up the matter at once.

Paka oma-tui means in Herero folk-lore to prick up the ears as an animal, properly, to move the ears *together*, to attend closely, to listen sharply, of which the later phrase *pakera m'omatui* (to put into one's ears, to listen) is a corruption. The origin and chain of thought as to Zulu *paka-ma* may therefore be traced as follows :—

Pa-Ka = to move quickly.

PA-KA = to move quickly *together*, hence

paka (*oma-tui*), to move the ears quickly together, as an animal, to raise the ears, listen attentively, "die ohren spitzen ;" from this *om-baka-tui*, attention; *e-patye* (for *e-pake*), an observant one; *paka-iza*, to look searchingly (like an animal with pricked-up ears; cf. with *paka* the widespread Aryan root *pas, spas, spek, späh, speh*, to look, to look searchingly, to examine, to *spy*) ;

paka-ma (Zulu), to be raised into a point, to stand erect, be high, elevated.

The same line of thought has been followed out in forming the Zulu nouns *in-taba*, mountain, hill, and *in-daba*, news—two words which seem to be perfect strangers to each other, but which nevertheless are closely allied, or, in fact, identical.

For the Bantu root TABA or TAVA primarily signifies to stretch horizontally, as the hand ; to stretch or strain generally ; to stretch or strain, as the udder or teats in milking (Herero *tava*); to stretch the head or the neck, as in close looking (Dutch *reikhalzen*), inspect closely (Herero *tav-iza*) ; to stretch the neck and prick up the ears, as an animal, to be attentive (to a call), to respond (*i-tav-era*) ; to listen to news, hence *in-daba* (Zulu), story, tale, news, report ; further, to raise into a point, be high, elevated, as the stretched neck and pricked-up ears of animals : hence Zulu *in-taba*, hill, mountain, properly point, allied to Herero *on-davi* or *oru-tavi*, point (of a plant or branch), ear of corn.

Or let us take the notion straight, right, just. The word for these conceptions is in Zulu *lunga*, primarily to move upward, raise erect. In Herero, where *ronga* (= *lunga*) has been employed for to prepare, get ready, equip (*rong-era*), the name for straight, right, just, is *semba*, primarily to outrun, to run as in a race, to run in a straight course, hence to be straight, right, just. In the Herero root *seka*, too, we have the vowel *e* (*i*) for a similar conception. *Seka* means now to equal, but originally it signified to outrun, to rival, as in a race, the primary meaning being still found in *ka-seka*, to distance, properly to run fast, far, to leave behind, as in racing. This combination of thought, namely, to race and to be straight, right, is very plain in Tshuana *sia*, identical with or allied to Herero *seka*. *Sia* means to run away (run fast, literally outrun), hence to win a race; *sia-na*, to race: hence *sia-ma*, to be running in a straight course, to be straight, right, just.

So it may also seem strange that in the Herero word for to drag (*koka*), to drag along the ground, the vowel *o* (*u*) should have been applied, and not *a*. The reason is, because some one or some thing must go *before* the object which is to be dragged, hence *koka* (indicat. *koko*), lit. to run or go *in front, before*, make follow, make a thing follow, drag it. Precisely the same intuition underlies the Konde synonym *uta*, to draw, and *uta-nga* (stronger form), to drag. Here we have the very same primary meaning, namely, to *go before*. *Uta* means in Herero to begin, properly to step in front before another, be the first, as in founding or cultivating a place. It is the parallel *u*-form of *yata* or *ata*, to step, tread :—

ata = to step, tread (on the ground);
uta (*utu*), to step before, to go ahead, before, to begin, be the first, found, create; but also (as in Konde) to go before a burden, *i.e.*, to drag.

Now the same line of thought we observe in the afore-mentioned Herero verb *koka* (*koko*). *Koka* (primitive form *KU-KU*) is the *u*-form of *kaka* = to run *on the ground*, to beat hard, as a road, or to run *together*, to congeal, become crusty, hard :—

kaka = to run on the ground or together (be or become hard, get a crust);
koka (*koko*), to run or go before (a burden), to make follow, drag.

In the Herero translation of the Psalms we read *n'otyinuino tyandye tyi tika*, and cup-mine-it-runneth over (Ps. xxiii. 5). The passage might also be translated *n'otyinuino tyandye tyi kona*, for *kona* (contracted form of *konda*) means to run over, to flow over (hence also to wash, wipe, cleanse, "reinigen"). Now the latter word (*kona*) substantiates our statement that the vowel *u . (o)* primarily means up, over; but how can *tika*, whose radical vowel *i* signifies in and from within, out, convey the same sense as *kona*? For the simple reason, because a flowing *out* may also be a flowing *over*. *N'otyinuino tyi tika* means literally "and my cup is running out," which is tantamount to "is running over." Hahn, in his "Herero Wörterbuch" says correctly, "*Tika* = aus- und überlaufen." For the primary sense is *out*, hence also *over*.

But *tika*, if doubled, means also to tickle (Zulu *tikatika*, Herero *tikatik-isa*). At first sight there does not seem to be any conceivable connection between the notions to run out or over, to overflow, and to tickle. But on closer examination we shall judge differently. Brincker leads us on the right track when he says, "*Tikatikisa* = kitzeln, eigentlich zum lachen reizen" (to tickle, properly to excite to laughter). Viewed in this light, the difficulty is at once removed. The literal meaning of *tikatika* (causative *tikatikisa*) is, to cause a pouring forth (of excessive laughter, as in tickling), hence to tickle.

Again, in Herero we have for the notion to lift up, to raise, both *yura* (*ura*) and *yera* (*era*). But how can the vowel *e* (*i*) in *yera* give the root the by-meaning *up*? Obviously because its original force is *out*, to outgo, exceed, hence also to *out*-lift, to *up*-lift, to raise :—

YURA, to go *up*, to lift *up*, raise, "aufheben ;"
YERA (YIRA), to outgo, exceed, lift *out* or up, "herausheben, empor-
 heben, aufheben."

In the following instances—predicative roots with the **primary** vague idea to run, to go—the evolution of thought is, on the whole, clearly seen, and speaks for itself.

HERERO.	PRIMARY SENSE.	DEVELOPMENT.
hanga	run together	assemble, form an alliance, enter into a covenant, make peace.

HERERO.	PRIMARY SENSE.	DEVELOPMENT.
yanga	run together	collect, as water in a periodical river or in holes; float on, as alluvial matter; collect, as one's thoughts, stand still, reflect, " sich zusammennehmen, sich sammeln."
handa	go or run on the ground	tread firmly, stem.
yanda	go or run on the ground	run fast; cease, end (run out of sight, disappear).
pata	go or run together	shut (as the two parts of a door, a trap, a box, &c.), catch (get close upon, be engaged in close fight, hence also) quarrel, contend, deny.
panda	go or run together	bind, fetter; work hard, be industrious (as a tied or tamed animal, *om-bandi*, or a bondsman).
vanda	go or run over the surface.	level, flatten, smooth, &c., spread (as a covering), cover.
mana (modified of *vanda*)	go or run over the surface	plaster (Konde *mata*), finish (originally a building by plastering), complete, bring to an end.
hiha	move to and fro	be moved with pity, sympathise, be desirous to provide for the wants of others, &c.
henga	run aside	shift, change.
tyiza	go in, between	discern, perceive.
heza	step out of the straight line	glide out, commit a mistake, fail.
henda	go out of the straight line, be oblique	be ambiguous (*omu-hendi*)

HERERO.	PRIMARY SENSE.	DEVELOPMENT.
tenga	outrun	be first, be respected, begin.
zenga	go or run in, between	(intercept, as with a snare), entangle.
vera (allied to *veta*)	run out (as a missile out of the hand)	(throw), beat, punish.
kuka	run up	start, travel.
koha	run over	wash, cleanse, purify, be pure, chaste.
hoha	run up	heap up, add.
huha	run round	(run round, as a rope), bind, fetter (by witchcraft), bewitch, bring misery upon one.
honga	run or go before	teach, good or bad, instigate.
kuta	go or run over	be full (of food), be satisfied.
suta	(cause to) run over	satisfy, pay, atone for.
kota	go down, bow	bow down, reverence, worship.
pora	go down, bow	be subdued, tame, calm, cool (as to temper), just, pious.

Herero *yazema*, to lend, to borrow, means literally to go or draw close together, to know each other well, as relatives or friends, to be on terms of intimacy, the root *yaze* or *aze* being identical with Zulu *azi*, to know (well, intimately), be kind to, regard, respect, be intimate: *mave yazema* (lit. they go close together, are closely connected, are intimate friends, hence) they lend, borrow.

The Herero verb *kuna*, to sow, to plant, primarily expresses the general and comprehensive idea to go before as a pioneer, to cultivate the ground, to found a place, to farm. For *kuna* is a contraction of *kunda*, which has in Herero the following meanings: (1.) to go or run up or over, to overflow, to be full (applied to numbers); (2.) to go before (as a herald), to make known in the villages, to announce (properly to herald); modified form: *kuna* = to go before, as a pioneer, be the first in cultivating a place, cultivate the ground, hence "to sow, to plant."

With Herero *kuna* we identify the Aryan root *KUN-* (*KON-*,

GAN-) in the O. Sax. *kun-ing*, Dutch *kon-ing*, Sansk. *ganaka* (in which the original *u* is changed to *a*), Engl. *king*,—and in Goth. *kuni*, O. Sax. *kunni*, Dutch *kunne*, Lat. *genus (genero)*, Engl. *kin*, relationship, family, &c. If the identity is admitted, we can in Bantu trace the primary meaning of *king* and *kin* as follows :—

KUN*a* (Herero ; contracted of *kunda ;* indicative form *kunu (KUNDU)* = (to *go before*, as a pioneer, be the first in cultivating a place), to farm, to plant, to sow ; (found a clan, beget, originate), create (Sansk. *gan* for a primitive *KUN-*) : hence

KUN-*ing* (king), first cultivator, founder of a place and family, progenitor, chief of a race or tribe, father, king (cf. Herero *omu-hona*, chief, lord, the stem *hona* being possibly a modified form of *kuna*) ;

KUN*i* (*kin*), generation, family, relationship.

We may here also, in conclusion, again point to the Herero verb *uta* (*utu*), most probably identical with, or allied to, the German *ur-* (in *ur-bar*, arable, being in a state of cultivation ; *ur-heber*, first beginner, author), in which we observe the very same train of thought, namely (1) to *step before*, to *go before* ; (2) to be the first, to begin ; and (3) to found, to originate, to create.

CHAPTER VIII.

ON THE HERERO PRONOUN — ABSOLUTE AND CONDI-TIONAL FORMS—PRIMEVAL LAW OF THE PLURAL—SEXUAL DUAL.

WE observe in Herero the following facts in connection with the pronoun :—

1. The pronouns, identical with the formative prefixes of the noun (treated in the Introduction to my English-Herero Dictionary), are *primitive nouns*, and mean—

    a. the living one (man, person, animal) ;
    b. the blowing, waving one (tree, branches, wings, waves, &c.) ;
    c. the dead one (tooth, bone, stone, earth) ;
    d. mother, female, mate (applied, in the first place, to living things, but also to dead things).

Examples.

u *u* = he or she (person) falls ;
u *u* = it (the tree) falls ;
ri *u* = it (the stone) falls ;
ru *u* = it (the rock) falls ;
tu *u* = they (the rocks) fall ;
mu *u* = (she) it (the grotto, house) falls.

Primitive form and literal sense.

KU u = the erect moving one (man) falls ;
PU u = the high waving one (tree) falls ;
TI u = the dead one (stone) falls ;
TU u the high dead one (rock) falls ;
THU u = the high dead ones (rocks) fall ;
MU u = the mother (womb-like place, grotto, house) falls.

2. Pronouns being thus in reality *nouns* with the meaning man, person, &c., the same pronoun may be used for representing the third and second, or even the first person, analogous to the Chinese " servant says " for " I say ; " as, for example :—

u *i* = he knows ;

u *i* = thou knowest.

Primitive form and literal sense.

KU i = (he) man know(s) ;

KU i = (thou) man know(est).

The above rule applies, however, only to those forms which represent man or woman, and whose consonants were originally *k*, *kh*, and *m*, *mh*. The originally dental forms (*ri*, *ru*, *tu*), and those who had for their primitive consonants *p*, *ph*, can, as they are names for inanimate things, only occur in the third person.

3. We distinguish two kinds of form in the pronoun—(*a*) the primitive, natural, or *absolute* form ; and (*b*) what we shall call the *conditional* form, because, under certain conditions relating to space and time, it is modified by the vowel-laws. The conditional is derived from the absolute form by change of vowel, the vowel *a* giving the pronoun the by-meaning *there*, yonder, distant, absent, abroad (third person) ; whilst the vowel *i*, by virtue of its meaning in, *in loco*, present, *here*, fits the pronoun for representing the first person or person present.

Examples.

KU (u) = man = he (absolute) ;

KA (a, e) = man = he there, absent, abroad (conditional).

Plural.

KHU (vu, u XIV.) = men = they (absolute, at present in use for abstract nouns) ;

KHA (va, ve, ba II.) = men = they *there* or abroad (conditional, at present used for men, people generally).

Now, as the conditional form for the third person is derived, by means of vowel-change, from the absolute ground-form, so is also the form for the first person obtained by changing the vowel *u* to *i*, as the following scheme shows :—

KU (u, **ku**) = man = he ; thou, thee (absolute).

KA (a, **ye**, e)	*KI* (*n*dyi, *n*gi, i)
= man *there*, absent, abroad	= man in loco, present, *here*
= he (conditional).	= I (conditional).

All the singular forms of the first person have, in Herero, the vowel *i*, or, contracted with the particles *a* and *ma*, *e*, viz., **ndyi** (**ngi**), **i**, **e** (= *a*-i), *me* (= *ma*-i), *a*mi (*a*-mi), *m*bi (*im*-**vi**). The latter form, though at present in general use for *I*, is originally first person plural, running parallel with the third person plural **va**, **ve** :—

KHU (**vu**, **u** in *o*u-*ndu*, humanity, originally) = men, people
= they (absolute).

KHA	*KHI*
(**va**, **ve**, *m*ba, *m*be) =	(**vi**, *m*bi) = men *here*, present
men *there*, abroad = they	= we (at present in use for
(conditional).	first person singular I).

4. *Primeval Law of the Plural.*—The plural of the Bantu primitive noun or pronoun was formed in accordance with the following simple law :—

In order to indicate the plural or a number of persons or things, aspirate the consonant of the singular, and pronounce the word with greater force.

Thus if *ka* meant the living one, *kha* denoted a number of living ones; if *ti* was the name for a dead body, as, *e.g.*, a tooth, a bone, a stone, *thi* conveyed the idea of a number of such dead bodies; and if *pu* signified the waving one, as a branch, a wing, a wave, the plural must have been something like *phu*. Later, when the primeval law of the plural became obsolete, a reaction took place; the massive plural forms collapsed by their own weight, and softened down— *kha* (or *khha*) to *tya, ta, za, ya, wa, va, ba, a*, &c. ; *khu* (or *khhu*) to *tyu, tshu, tu, yu, wu, bu, u*, &c. In these and similar shapes the plural forms appear at present in Bantu. Thus the plural of **ru**, **lu** (*TU*) XI., originally *thu* or *thhu*, is now (in Herero) **tu** XII., and in the corresponding demonstrative pronoun **su**; both the singular and the plural have lost a grade of their original power : **tu** having been weakened to **ru** (**lu**), and *thu* or *thhu* to **tu** or **su**. The present plural prefix **vi-** VIII. (**wi-, hi-, iy-, i-**), to add another instance, is only a weak remnant of an original *khi* or *khhi*, the plural of **ki-** VII. (**tyi-, si-, y-, i-**). See the pronominal tables in the Introduction to my English-Herero Dictionary, and at the end of Chapter X.

5. This leads us to call attention to the *modification of consonants* in the various forms of the primitive noun (prefix) and pronoun, especially in the plural—changes which can still be traced in Herero to their natural cause. We observe that gutturals have changed, on the one hand, to dentals, and, on the other, to labials, as *e.g.* the primitive plural form *KHA :*—

$$KHA = \text{living beings} = \text{they.}$$

va II. = they (men).	**za** X. = they (animals, &c.)

In Kihiau the forms of the VIII. class of nouns are **vi** (**wi**) and **hi**, the latter betraying its descent from an original *KHI*. In Ndonga we have *po-hi*, on the earth, *i.e.*, beneath (Herero *p-e-hi*), but *e-vi*, earth (Herero *e-hi*), *h* having changed to *v*. As to the transition in Bantu from *kh*, *ty*, *dy*, to *z*, this is the same as the change in Greek from *dy* to *z*,—Sanskrit *Dyaus*, for example, being in Greek *Zeus*.

In the same way as **va** II. and **za** X. from *KHA*, the plural pronoun **tu** (Tshuana **cho, tsho**), we, us, was derived from an original *KHU*, the connecting link (*thu, tshu, tsho, tyu*) being still in existence in Herero and other Bantu idioms :—

$$KHU = \text{living, erect moving beings} = \text{men (absolute form).}$$

vu, u, bu (orig. = men) = they (absolute form).	**tu** = men = we, us (absolute form).

Here we see that the third and first persons (plural) are represented by forms essentially one. But it must be borne in mind that in the XIV. class of nouns and pronouns two (or perhaps three) classes have coalesced, viz., the primitive form *PU* (**u, vu, bu,** sing. XIV.), and *KHU* (**u, vu, bu,** plur. XIV.) = men (absolute), at present in use as a diminutive plural and also as a singular for abstract nouns. All the abstract nouns with the prefix *o*u- (**vu, bu** XIV.) must be regarded as adjectives of *o*u-*ndu* (**vu**-*ndu* = *KHU-ndu*), at present denoting humanity, but originally men, people (absolute form), of which the conditional form *o***va**-*ndu* (**ba**-*ntu* = *KHA-ntu*) is an offshoot :—

*o*u-*ndu* (**bu**-*ntu* = *KHU-ntu*) humanity, properly men, people (absolute);

*o***va**-*ndu* (**ba**-*ntu* = *KHA-ntu*), men there, abroad (conditional).

The original meaning, therefore, of Herero *o*ŭ-*ninga-ndu* (happiness) is happy men; of *o*ŭ-*haze-ndu* (negligence), negligent people; of *o*u-*pore* (gentleness, righteousness, piety), righteous, good men, &c., just as the ending -*head*, -*hood* (in manhood, knighthood) also appears to have primarily signified "person."

Shifting of Nouns.—It is particularly interesting to observe in Herero how a concrete noun, after coming into use as an abstract, was replaced by another. Sometimes the new concrete noun was merely a modification of the old one, but in other cases an entirely new name was coined. Thus *o*ŭ-*ndu* denoted, as we have seen, originally men (absolute), and on becoming an abstract (viz., humanity), it was replaced by the conditional form *o***va**-*ndu*, men, people (properly people abroad). *O***mi**-*tuka* (r. *tuka*, start up, fly) was one of the original names for wings, but on assuming the character of an abstract in "levity," another word (*o***tyi**-*vava*, outspread thing) was chosen to take its place. *O***n**-*dyoze*, originally the twisting, spinning animal, probably spider, from *yoza*, to twist, spin (allied to *o***n**-*goze*, cord), means at present phantom, vision, "traumbild," literally twisted thing, answering exactly to the German "(hirn)gespinnst." ' Its substitute is *o***ty**-*auvi*, spider. The original Bantu name for goat is (Zulu) *i***m**-*buzi* (identical with the Herero abstract *o***m**-*buze*, news, rumour, report, inquisitiveness) = the prying, inquisitive, curious animal, from *buza* (Herero *pura*), to inquire, ask about news, be inquisitive. Now when *o***m**-*buze* (= *i***m**-*buzi*), the inquisitive, curious animal, came to mean "news, rumour, report (curiosity)," the present name for goat, *o***n**-*gombo*, was adopted.

HERERO NOUNS.	ORIGINAL CON-CRETE SENSE.	ABSTRACT SENSE.	PRESENT SUBSTI-TUTE.
*o*u-*ndu*	men	humanity	*o*va-*ndu*, men.
*o*mi-*tuka*	wings	levity	*o*tyi-*vava*, wing.
*o*n-*dyoze*	spinning ani-mal (spider ?)	phantom	*o*ty-*auvi*, spider.
*o*m-*buze*	goat	news (curio-sity)	*o*n-*gombo*, goat.
*o*n-*dyoura*	elephant	abundance	*o*n-*dyou*(*ra*), ele-phant.

After this digression it may be convenient to briefly sum up the *evidence for the primeval law of the plural.*

(1.) Dr. Bleek says ("Comparative Grammar," p. 145) :—" The whole system of substituting a plural prefix for a singular one " (as *o*ru-*vio*, knife, *o*tu-*vio*, knives) " is certainly older than that of adding a particle indicating the plural to the form of a singular prefix " (as *o*u-*ta*, bow, *o*ma-u-*ta*, bows).   Now if this be so—and no true Bantu scholar will contradict it—then we are forced to the conclusion, considering the perfect harmonious regularity we everywhere meet with in Bantu, that there must be some *innate connection* between the singular form and its plural substitute.

(2.) The *existence* of such a connection is plain from the fact that, for example, a singular *k* in Herero, in whatever vowel-colour it may appear in the domain of the pronoun, invariably takes the consonants *v* (*w*) and *z* (whose easy interchange is obvious in in-stances like Herero *ovi-* VIII. and Zulu *izi-* VIII., Herero *on-*(D)*zu* and Zulu *im-vu*, sheep) for its plural substitutes, whilst the singular *r* (*l*) changes into the cognate dental *t :*—

omu-ndu (**k**u-mu-ndu), man   *o*va-*ndu*, men.
u (**k**u), he, she (man)   **v**e, they (men).
*o*tyi-*puka* (**ki**-puka), wild animal *o*vi-*puka*, wild animals.
ty*i* (**ki**), it   **v***i*, they (things).
ke, it (diminutive)   *u* (**v**u), they.
i (**ki**), he, she, it (animal)   **z**e, they (animals, &c.).
*o*ru-*vio*, knife   *o*tu-*vio*, knives.
r*u*, it   **t***u*, they.

(3.) Now it is especially the latter correspondence, *r* in **ru** XI.
taking for its plural substitute the stronger dental *t* in **tu** XII.,
which throws light on the *nature* of the original connection between
the singular and plural forms. It consists simply in this, that in
indicating the plural, the consonant of the singular was pronounced
with stronger emission of breath and greater force. Thus the
singular *ru* (*TU*) became the plural *tu* (*THU*), and the singulars
ka, tyi (*KI*), *u* (*KU*) changed into plural forms by assuming such
consonants as *kh* or *khh*, which in course of time degenerated to
sounds like *v, b, w, z*. The easy transition from a guttural to a
labial is obvious from examples like Herero *-haze* (negligent, dis-
orderly) and the identical Zulu *-vazi* (scattered, neglected) ; Bantu
-kazi (female) and Kafir (*um*)*-fazi* (wife, woman), also from English
words ending in *gh*, as trough, rough, enough, which are now
pronounced trof, ruf, enuf.

Here a word of caution may not be out of place. Care must be
taken not to confound the prefix **tu-**, which in Angola and some
other idioms corresponds as plural to **ka-** XIII., with the above-
mentioned **tu-** (*THU*) XII., the original and legitimate plural of
ru- (*TU*) XI. The Angola prefix *o*tu-, as plural of *o*ka-, is only a
phonetic variation of the identical Herero prefix *o*u (*o*vu-) XIV.,
both being derived from the primitive absolute form 9 *KHU*.
Angola *o*tu- stands to Herero *o*(v)u- in the same relation as Zulu
*i*zi- VIII. to Herero *o*vi- VIII., and ought to be marked, according
to Bleek's classification of the prefixes, *o*tu- (*KHU*) XIV., and not
*o*tu- (*THU*) XII. The Bantu pronoun 1st. pers. plur. **tu** (orig. *KHU*
= persons, or *we*) is therefore identical with the ·Angola plural
prefix *o*tu- (*THU* = *KHU* = **vu** = living things, answering to the
singular **ka-** XIII., orig. living thing), whilst it is radically different
from the homophonous Herero *o*tu- (*THU*) XII., which corresponds to
*o*ru- (*TU*) XI., and means, as we stated before, rising, high, long
dead things. Angola *o*(v)u- and *o*tu-, like Herero *o*va- and *o*zo-*n*-,
are variations of one common root, the dental element having been
introduced in Angola *o*tu-, in order to distinguish this prefix from
the abstract *o*(v)u-. As a consequence, however, the *real* Herero
and Kongo **tu-** XII. was lost in Angola.

(4.) We have already drawn attention, in Chapter VI., to the
analogy of the consonantal change in the verb, *greater force being*

E

expressed by a stronger letter, intransitive verbs being made transitive or causative by substituting an aspirate for a tenuis, though these aspirates were afterwards reduced to fricatives,—*kh*, for example, to *v* and *z*, exactly as we find it in the pronominal roots. The derivative (frequentative) verb *rambuka*, for instance, means to be thin, lean (r. *ramba*, drive away, pursue, chase), but *rambuza* (orig. *rambutha = rambukha*) is to *make* thin, to *cause* to be lean ; *kutuka* means unbound, but *kutura* (= *kutuza = kututha = kutukha*), to unbind. Now here we have the operation of the same law which formed from the Zulu singular *isi*- VII. (*KI*) the plural *izi*- VIII. (Herero *ovi*-, orig. *KHI*), or from the Herero singular *on*- (Zulu *in*-, orig. *KI-MI*) the plural *ozo-n*- (Zulu *i-zi-n*-, full form *KHA-KI-MI*).

(5.) Additional collateral evidence we have in the numerical correspondence in the pronouns of our own languages, the guttural *k* (*h*) in the pronouns of the first and third persons *I* (*KI*) and *he* (*KU* or *KA*) having changed to plural *we* (*wi*, orig. *KHI*) and *they* (orig. *THA = KHA*).

It would thus seem that the restoration of the following numerical Herero correspondences to their primitive full form is warranted by sufficient proof :—

Singular.	Plural.
omu-ndu (**ku**-mu-ndu) man.	*ova-ndu* (**kha**-ndu), men.
u (**ku**), he, she (man).	*ve, va* (**kha**), they (men).
on-gombe (**ki**-mi-kombe), ox or cow.	*ozon - gombe* (**tha**-ki-mi-kombe = **kha**-ki-mi-kombe), cattle.
i (**ki**), he, she, it (animal).	*ze, za* (**tha** = **kha**), they (animals, &c.)
otyi-rongo (**ki**-rongo), a habitable place.	*ovi-rongo* (**khi**-rongo), habitable places.
tyi (**ki**), it.	**vi** (**khi**), they.
oka-na, a little thing.	*ou-na* (**khu**-na), little things.
ke, ka, it.	**u, vu** (**khu**), they.
oru-vio (**tu**-vio), knife.	*otu-vio* (**thu**-vio), knives.
ru (**tu**), it.	**tu** (**thu**), they.

6. *Gender—Sexual Dual.*—There are three different kinds of gender in the primitive noun or pronoun, viz. :—

(*a*.) The *common personal gender*, denoting living beings, without reference to sex, also used for the *masculine gender :*

KU = living one, man = he, person (common gender and masculine).

(*b.*) A distinct *feminine gender* to distinguish females or mates of
beings and things appearing in pairs :

MU = mother, woman, mate = she (feminine gender).

(*c.*) The *sexual dual*, male and female united as one, couple, pair :

KU-MU = man-wife = they, the two in one, the human pair
(sexual dual).

It would appear that in the primitive language all breathing,
living beings, whether male or female, were treated alike. They
were spoken of indiscriminately as living beings or creatures.
Viewed separately, a young man and a young woman, a young
male and a young female animal, might be designated by the same
name, meaning the living one, the living thing. It was only when
the living beings or creatures, in mature age, appeared in pairs
that the grammatical distinction of gender was resorted to, and the
forms of the sexual dual were used, denoting male and female
united. Now, if one of the united pair had to be named separately,
the form of the common gender (*KU, KI, KA*) was used for desig-
nating the male, whilst the distinct feminine form (*MU, MI, MA*)
was applied to the female.

And as to inanimate things, primeval man, in viewing and
naming them, did not ask, " Is the thing in any way like a male—
big, strong, hard, active; or like a female—smaller, weaker, soft,
passive ? "—questions belonging to a later period; but, " Is the
object like a living thing (with life, blood, as arm, leg, ear) ? " or,
" Is it waving like wings or branches moved by the wind ? " or,
" Is the thing motionless, dead (like bones, horns, stones) ? " The
single horn, for example, of a one-horned rhinoceros would not
suggest to him the idea of gender; he would simply call the isolated
horn a dead one or a dead thing; but observing on many other
animals two horns standing together, the second one would appear
to him as the female or mate of the first, and thus comparing them
to a married couple, he would accordingly classify the pair of horns,
though lifeless objects, like pairs of living beings, in one of the
classes of the sexual dual.

Now when, in the long lapse of ages, the original meaning of the sexual dual, "the being (or thing) and its mate," or "male *and* female," was lost, the idea "male *or* female" was substituted, and so it happened that the dual form was applied to males or females indiscriminately, in the same way as also our *man, mensch,* denotes man in general, "male *and* female," but also "male *or* female." We have in Bantu the germ of what is more extensively developed in the so-called sex-denoting languages.

Evidence for the Sexual Dual.—(Cf. §§ 10–25 of the Introduction to my English-Herero Dictionary.)

(1.) The existence, in Bantu, of *double* formative prefixes, properly compounded primitive nouns (something like the Chinese *fu mu* = father-mother = parents), which originally must have denoted a *double* object, a *couple.*

(2.) The dualistic tendency of the compound prefix *o*ma-, *KA-MA*, first observed in Herero by the Rev. J. Rath : *oma-* being applied as plural for most things which appear *in pairs,* as *ome-ho,* eyes (properly the pair of eyes, male and female), *oma-ke* (the two) hands, *oma-oko* (the two) arms, *oma-rama* (the two) legs, &c.

(3.) The radical identity of the two prefixes for those classes of nouns in which *natural* gender is observed, *o*mu-, *KU-MU*, I. (man), *o*n, *o*m-, *KI-MI*, IX. (animal), with the dualistic prefix *o*ma-, *KA-MA*, VI., the radical identity of these three forms being placed beyond doubt by the corresponding demonstrative pronouns :—

PREFIX.	NOUN.	PERS. PRON.	DEMONSTR. PRON.
*o*ma- (*KA-MA*).	*o*ma-*oko,* arms (orig. sexual dual, male and female,' *i.e.,* right and left arm).	e (*KA*).	*in-*ga (*INI-KA*).
*o*n- (*KI-MI*).	*o*n-*gombe,* ox *or* cow (orig. sexual dual, ox *and* cow).	i (*KI*).	*in-*dyi (*INI-KI*).
*o*mu- (*KU-MU*).	*o*mu-*ndu,* man, person, male *or* female (orig. sexual dual, male *and* female).	u (*KU*).	*in-*gui (*INI-KU*).

(4.) The identity of the Bantu primitive nouns *HI*, father, and *NI*, mother, with the compound formative prefix *o*n- or *i*n- (*KI-MI*) :—

$$in\text{- (IX. prefix)} =$$
$$KI \ - \ MI.$$
$$\| \quad | \quad \|$$
$$HI, \quad NI,$$

father, | mother,
male. | female.

(5.) The peculiar character of the Herero noun *o***mu**-*tena* = brother of a sister, or sister of a brother, which originally must have denoted brother *and* sister, " geschwister-paar."

(6.) The fact that *o***mu**- III., though at present a singular prefix, is used for representing the *two finger-rows* or the number *ten*. *Omu-rongo* means ten in Herero. The word is compounded of the singular prefix *omu-* III. and the adjectival stem *-rongo*, from *ronga* (in *rongera*), to make straight, get ready, prepare, equip. The prefix *omu-* evidently refers here to the same object as *omu-nue*, namely, finger. The proper meaning of *omu-rongo* is, therefore, the ready or skilled *omu-* or finger. I think there can be no doubt that *omu-rongo* is one of the original Bantu names for finger. But would the word have been employed for representing the number *ten* if originally it denoted only *one* finger ? Not even if its meaning had been one finger-*row*, for that would have only been *five*. The fact is, the full form and original meaning of *omu-rongo* is *PU-MU-RONGO* = the ready, skilled, wing-like (or branch-like) pair, that is, the *two rows of fingers*, that is, *ten*.

(7.) It is also worthy of note that in Suto (and probably other dialects) the right hand or arm is called the *male* (*letsogo le letona*) and the left the female hand (*letsogo le letshegali*), which seems to indicate that, although the sexual dual, as such, is extinct in Bantu, yet the primitive intuition underlying it is not quite obliterated from the mind of the people.

7. Some of the primitive pronominal forms have, through the wear and tear of ages, been reduced to single vowels. Of the primitive dual form *KA-MA*, for instance, only the first vowel is left in the Herero personal pronoun *a* (*ka-ma*), and even that is changed

to *e*, though in the corresponding demonstrative pronoun *nga* the first part, *ka* (**ka**-*ma*), has been preserved. Some of the pronouns of different classes or genders of nouns have coalesced; others have shifted from one class to another, but their wanderings can still be traced. Also, by tampering with number and case, the grand primitive system has suffered : dual and plural forms have come into use as singulars, and genitive forms have taken their place in the nominative. *M*bi (**vi**), for example, at present = *I*, is properly, as we saw already, the parallel *i*-form of *m*ba (**va**) = these, those (people), and meant originally *we ;* and *a*mi = of me, mine, me, stands now in Herero in the nominative for *I*.

For a complete statement of the Herero pronominal forms (prefixes and pronouns), the student is referred to my English-Herero Dictionary (Cape Town and London), and to Table III. at the end of Chapter X.

CHAPTER IX.

THE OPERATION OF COMMON LAWS TRACEABLE IN THE BANTU AND ARYAN PRONOUNS.

IT is, I believe, generally admitted that the pronouns belong to the most ancient forms in language, and that, for this reason, their etymology is enveloped in much darkness and doubt. It would seem there is not a single personal pronoun in the Aryan and Semitic families whose etymology has been established as perfectly certain. All the labour bestowed and all the learning brought to bear upon this subject appear to have resulted in nothing but the unanimous confession of those best able to judge that "the etymology of the Aryan personal pronouns is doubtful,—that they are words which for the present must remain without a genealogy."

And so they would have to remain for ever, were it not that a family of languages has been discovered in Africa which has preserved about twice, if not three times, as many genuine pronominal roots as are found either in the Semitic or Aryan languages. The time is probably not far distant when it will be accepted as a fact that the pronouns of the latter and other families are based on the very same principles as the pronominal forms in Bantu. The changes and shiftings of sound are, of course, considerable, but as to the first and second person, we have the advantage of knowing that, in all families of speech, they can only be derived from those absolute forms which mean, in the primitive language, the erect moving living one, man (*KU*, plur. *KHU*), and the erect moving mother or female (*MU*, plur. *MHU*). A dental or lingual in Aryan, Semitic, and other families, *may* be original in the *third* person, but if found in the first and second, as, *e.g.*, Hottentot *ta*, *tita*, I, Lat. *tu*, Germ. *du* (*thou*); we know that the dentals *t*, *d*, *th* have been substituted for the original guttural *k*, plural *kh*. Or when we find that in Hebrew the separate pronoun of the 2nd. pers. sing. is ATAH = thou, we know that this is only a variation of the more primitive form retained for the accusative (or verbal suffix) KA = thee, radically identical with or closely allied to HUA = he, HU = him. The identity of Herero *n*dyi (*n*gi), i, *KI* (= man present, 1st. pers. sing.) and English *I* (Goth. *ik*) ; of Makonde we-*pa*, *KHI* (= men present, 1st. pers. plur.) and English *we* (Swed. *vi*) ; of Herero *e*ye, ye, *KA, KU* (3rd. pers. sing.) and English *he*, and other forms, can hardly be doubted.

But let us proceed methodically, in accordance with the principles set forth in the preceding chapters, and tentatively trace the identity of some of the most important forms of the pronoun in Bantu and Aryan.

Principles of Comparison.—It will be expedient, at the outset, to briefly premise the points which in any attempt to identify pronouns of different families must form the basis of research.

1. No pronoun stands isolated in any language ; it is in all cases a member of a group, and must be treated as such.

2. A personal pronoun is properly a *primitive noun*, meaning *man, person*, &c., or, in feminine forms, *mother, woman, female ;* one and the same absolute form may stand, therefore, for the second and third, or even for the first person. In the primitive language, the sentence "man goes" signified both "he goes" and "thou goest." That, for example, the Hebrew -NU means *our*, and the Herero -NU signifies *your* (plur.), is no reason why the two pronouns should not be identical.

3. There are, however, conditional forms for the first and third person, so called because they have by-meanings referring to space and locality, the form for the first person assuming, as a rule, the vowel *i* = here, present, whilst in the third person we find the absolute *u*-form changed to *a* (*e*) = there, at some distance, abroad.

4. All pronouns representing *man* have originally the guttural *k* (common gender and masculine), plural *kh ;* and for the feminine gender the labial *m*, plur. *mh*. To these primitive letters the various consonants of the first and second person in universal speech, however adventurous their career may have been, must be traced. The third person, including as it does inanimate things, has also the other primitive consonants *t*, plur. *th*, and *p*, plur. *ph*.

5. Originally the feminine gender was distinguished, not only in the third and second, but also in the first person, and sometimes the feminine form, if lost in the nominative, reappears in other cases. Sanskrit *mâ* (-*mi*) and *aham*, for instance, are not variations of one common root, as some hold, but two distinct pronouns, the first of the originally feminine and the latter of the common personal (and masculine) gender. Bopp points out clearly that the -*am* in *aham* is merely an ending and inorganic. " Das *am* von *aham*," he says, " ist endung, wie in *tvam*, du, *ayam*, dieser, und *svayam*, selbst, und wie im plural *vayam*, wir, *yuyam*, ihr. Der nominativ I. pers. sing. ist von anderm stamme als die obliquen casus." In Herero we have an analogous case : besides *me* (*ma*-i = *ma-KI*), I, we find also the form *a*mi I, me, in which the labial is radical ; in *me* it is inorganic. *Me* is common personal and masculine, but *a*mi, though at present also common gender, was primarily feminine. Now as Herero *me* (*ma*-i, *ma-KI*) corresponds to Skr. *a*-h-*am*, Goth. *i*-k ; so the Skr. accusative **mâ**, **mâm** (**ma**-*am*), and the nominative verbal suffix -**mi**, I, correspond to Herero *a*-**mi**, I, me :—

KU

= man, person (absolute form).
Common personal and masculine, at present common, gender.

Bantu.	Aryan.
ki (Tshuana), *n***dyi, i,** *m*e (Herero) = man here, person present = I.	*i***k** (Goth. and Dutch), *i*ch (Germ.), *e*go (Lat. and Gr.), *a*-**h**-*am* for *agam* (Skr.), **I.**

Feminine, at present common gender.

a-**mi** (Bantu), I, me : *MI* signifying originally mother, woman, or female *here* = I, me.	-**mi** (Skr.), as in *as*-**mi**, Engl. *a*-**m**, I am ; **m**â, **mâm**, **ma**-*am* (Skr.), me, **mi**-*k* (Goth. and Icel.), **mi** (Low Germ.), **me.**

6. The primeval law of the pronominal plural is the same as that of the primitive nouns (or Bantu prefixes). It is, as we saw before, of an extremely simple nature : the consonant of the singular is aspirated and strengthened, the singular *k*, for example, becom-

ing plural *kh* or *khh*, the latter originally strong plural consonant appearing in its present collapsed state in the several families as *w, v, b, th, z,* &c.

7. Sometimes the plural is substituted for the singular, as an original *we* for *I*.

8. The question of case is of no moment in investigations into the nature and identity of pronouns. Originally any pronoun, in virtue of its character as a primitive noun, could stand in any case. The present fixed use of certain forms for certain cases is purely conventional.

9. In some pronouns, as we know them now, two or more forms have coalesced.

10. I would also draw attention to what I consider an interesting discovery in Bleek's " Comparative Grammar " (pp. 150, 151), viz., that the vowel (or article) which precedes a Bantu formative prefix, as in Zulu *u*lu-, *i*li-, is in its origin *a pronoun and identical with the prefix which it precedes.* In other words, the primitive article in Bantu is formed from the prefix of the noun (or pronominal root) which it precedes, by suppressing the consonant and retaining only the radical vowel, as *u*-lu- XI. from *lu*-lu-, *a*ba- II. from *ba*-ba-, &c. ; and, we further add, if the prefix was a compound, as *u*-mu- I. (*KU-MU*), *u*-mu- III. (*PU-MU*), the second syllable, *-mu-, -ma-*, &c., was elided in the article. Thus not *kumu-KUMU-* I., but *ku-KUMU* (afterwards *u*-umu-, *u*-mu- I.) ; not *pumu-PUMU-*, but *pu-PUMU-* (at present *u*-umu-, *u*-mu- III.).

Now it appears to me that there are some traces left in Bantu and in the Aryan languages to show that the primitive article, discovered by Bleek in the Bantu noun, also may be found to precede and emphasise *a pronoun* in all genders, numbers, and persons. Bleek has shown that Zulu *i*-si- VII. = *a* THING or *the* THING, was originally *si*-si = *thing*-THING (*this* or *the* THING), that *u*-(*u*)mu- I. = *a* MAN or *the* MAN, was in the ancient language *man*-MAN (*this* or *the* MAN). Now, it would seem possible, or even probable, that, for example, the vowel *i* which precedes the radical *k* in Goth. *i*K (I), and the prefixed *u* in Goth. *u*-GK-*is* (us two), may have been originally identical respectively with K(I), I, and GK(U), us, so that the full form and meaning of Goth. *IK* and *UGK-* may have been—

ki-KI = *man here-MAN HERE* = *i-KI* = *i*ᴋ = *this* ᴍᴀɴ here (I).
khu-KHU = *men-MEN* = *u-KHU* = *u*ɢᴋ- = *these* ᴍᴇɴ (a number,
  or only two, we, us).

Another illustration. The Kongo prefix *eye*- (in *eye-kala* V.,
human being, plur. **a**-*kala* II.) and the Herero separate pronoun
eye, he, she, properly this or that person (with which the Skr.
a-**y**-*am*, this one, may be compared) are radically identical. Now
the initial *e*- (Skr. *a*-) is the primitive or (as we may call it in
honour of its discoverer) *Bleek's article.* Its force is " this, that,
the : "—**ye** = he or person there : *e*-**ye**, (*y*)*e*- **ye** = (*k*)*e*-**ke** (primarily
ka-KA) = that (this or the) person there, *the*-he or *the*-she :—

eye-kala (Kóngo), human being, lit. that (this or the) human being ;
eye (Herero), he, she, properly *the* he, or *that* person there ;
a-**y**-*am* (Sanskrit), this one.

It would therefore appear that there was a period in language
when there were as many articles (or demonstrative pronouns) as
there are primitive nouns (or personal pronouns), namely, forty-
three (see Table II.). But it is self-evident that this state of things
could not last : in course of time the primitive articles lost their
power, and became part of the primitive noun or pronoun, as, for
example, Zulu *ulu*- (for *lu* **lu**), Goth. *i***k**(i), I (for *ki* **ki**) ; and only
one or two of the large number survived, which were now generally
applied in all cases. These forms, as, *e.g.*, Bantu *a*-, the Semitic *ha*,
hal, al, and the Aryan *ta, sa, the,* we shall call secondary articles.
Very frequently the primitive and the secondary article have
blended in Bantu into one sound, as Herero *oru*- (for *a-u*-**ru**-), *otu*-
(for *a-u*-**tu**), Kongo *e*-**ki**- (for *a-i*-**ki**), *eri*- (for *a-i*-**ri**), &c.

11. But there are other particles besides the primitive article
which stick to the pronoun as limpets to a rock, as, for example,
the prefixed *in*-, (*i*)*n*-, in Herero (*i*)*n***dyi**, I, *ingui*, this one, Hebrew
an-, *en*-, in *ano***ki**, I, *en***hu**, him, and the Sansk. ending -*am* in *a***h**am, I,
yû*yam*, you. In Bantu these particles fall into three classes : (*a*.)
demonstrative or emphasising particles, as *in*- in Herero (*i*)*n***dyi**, I,
properly this self-I, I myself, *ingui*, this one, this self-same one ; (*b*.)
case-particles, as *a*- in *a***mi**, I, of I, of me, mine, hence also me and
I ; (*c*.) tense-indicating particles, as *ma*- in *ma***tu**, we (present and

future tense) = we on the spot, we here present; **tu***a*, we (past
tense) = we there, at a distance, in the past. Some of the latter
kind can still be separated from the root, as *ma*- from *ma***tu**, *a*- from
*a***tu**, *a***ve**, but as to the emphasising particles, they have, as in other
families, grown together with the pronoun into one word, as, *e.g.*,
Konde **mi***pa* (**mi**-*pa*), I, properly I (near or) here.

Affinities between the Aryan and Bantu Personal Pronoun.—Let us
now briefly glance at the personal pronouns **I** (Goth. and Dutch *i***k**,
Skr. *a*ham), plural **we** (O. Sax. **wi**, Swed. **vi**, Skr. **va***yam*); **thou**
(Lat. and Pers. **tu**, Germ. **du**, Skr. **tv***am*, **tu***am*), plur. **you** (Dutch
u, Skr. **yû***yam*); **he** (Sax. **he**, O. Engl. **ha**, **a**), plur. **they** (O. Sax.
thâ, Goth. **thá***i*), and compare them with corresponding forms in
Bantu.

We begin with the singular pronoun of the second person, **thou**
(Lat. **tû**).

Here the primitive vowel *u* has been preserved, but the dental
consonant is a changed *k*, the original form being the Bantu *KU* =
the living, erect moving one = man = thou. *Thou*, therefore, is properly (thou) *man*. The original *k* we have in the first person *i***k** (I),
and approximately (*h* being so near akin to *k*), in the third person
he. *Tu* (*thou*), like Bantu **ku** (thee), by aphæresis **û** (thou), is the
absolute form of the common personal pronoun (singular), simply
meaning *man*, without reference to person or place. Thus "thou
sayest" is properly "man says," just as the Herero "*u tya*"
means both "he says" and "thou sayest," because its literal sense
is "*man* says."

Now, from this form *tu* = *ku* is derived, by aspirating and
strengthening the consonant, the plural **you** (*guw*, *yû*-*yam*), originally *KHU* or *KHHU*, which in Bantu has assumed the forms **tu**,
tyu, **tshu** (1st. pers. plur.) and **vu**, **u** (3rd. pers. sing. and plur.,
orig.) = *KHU* = men (absolute form) :—

SINGULAR.	PLURAL.
thou (Lat. **tu**) =	**you** (O. Engl. **guw**) =
KU = man	*KHU* = men
(absolute).	(absolute).

Bantu.

ku; u : thee ; thou,
he, properly
KU = man
(absolute).

tu (tyu, tshu) =
KHU = (we) men
(absolute).

We further observe that from the above two absolute forms *KU* and *KHU* proceed by change of vowel—

(*a.*) the first person I, Goth. *ik*, Zulu *n*gi, Herero *n*dyi, i (in *me* = *ma*-i), Kafir *n*di, Tshuana **ki** = *KI* = man here, man present = *I*—

From this the plural, in accordance with the law stated before : **we**, O. Sax. and Low Germ. **wi**, Swed. **vi**, originally *KHI*, the corresponding Bantu forms being Konde **we***pa*, Herero *m***bi** (= *m*-**vi**, I, but properly *we*), Zulu **ti, tsi, si**, Herero *e*te (= *THI* = *KHI*) = *we*.

(*b.*) The third person, or person there, at some distance, abroad, absent, **he**, Bantu *e*ye, e, **ka**, a, primitive form *KA*—

From which is derived the plural **they**, O. Sax. **thâ**, Goth. **thá***i* = *KHA* = (they) men there, abroad, absent = Bantu **va (ve) ba** (they II.), and collaterally **za, ze** (they X. Herero), as the subjoined comparative table shows :—

ENGLISH PERSONAL PRONOUNS.

thou (tu) = KU = man (absolute form).

a.

I (*ic*, *ik*) = KI = (I) man *here* (conditional form).   he (ha, a) = KA = (he) man *there* (conditional form).

Plural.

yoñ = KHU = (you) men (absolute form).

we (wi) = KHI = (we) men *here* (conditional form).   they (thai) = KHA = (they) men *there* (conditional form).

CORRESPONDING FORMS IN HERERO.

ku, u = KU = (thee, thou) man (absolute form).

i,   *a.*

ndyi, i (ki, ngi) = KI = (I, me), man *here* (conditional form).   eye, e, (ka), a = KA = (he, she), man *there* (conditional form).

Plural.

u, vu (XIV.) = KHU = abstract, but orig. (they) men (absolute form).

mbi (*m-vi*), I, orig. we; Konde we-(*pa*) = KHI = men *here*, we (conditional form);—

ve, va (ba), II. = KHA = (they) men *there* (conditional form);—

Collateral form in which KHI is changed to THI: Collateral form in which KHA is changed to THA:

ti, ete (tsi, si) = THI = KHI = men *here*, we.   ze, za (tha) X. = THA = KHA = (they) living things *there*, or, *at large.*

Review of the English Personal Pronoun.

I (*KI*).

Fuller form Goth. and Dutch *ik*, German *ich*, Lat. and Gr. *ego*. As no primitive root can end with a consonant, the original form of **I** must have been *iKI*, analogous to Hebrew *an-o-***ki**, (Bantu) Tshuana **ki**, Zulu *n*gi, Herero *n*dyi, Xosa *n*di, in which latter form the guttural is changed to a dental, as also in Nama (Hottentot) **tit**a. The radical vowel *i*, which has become mute in *i*k', *i*k(i), has been preserved in the corresponding plural **we**, Dan. and Swed. **wi or vi**, originally *KHI*. The initial vowel *i* in Goth. *i*k we take to be the primitive or Bleek's article. The full form and meaning of *ik*, I, is therefore probably

$$kiKI = i\mathbf{ki} = \text{this man here (or self)},$$

7*a KI* being the conditional *i* form of 7*KU* = the grown-up, erect moving one, man (absolute).

The predilection of Sanskrit for the *a*-sound has probably been the cause of changing the primitive *i*, so essential in the first person, into *a*. *Aham* (*a-h-am*) appears to be a combination of the following three parts :—

(*a.*) The radical **h'**, a remnant of 7*a KI* = man here ;-

(*b.*) Bleek's article *a-* (for an original *i*) = *this* or *the* (man here); and

(*c.*) The ending -*am*.

ME (*MI*).

Goth. and Icel. *mik*, O. Germ. *mih*, Skr. *mâm*, *mâ*, objective case of I, myself. The ending -*ik*, -*k*, -*ch*, -*h* in the Teutonic languages, and -*am* (*yam*, *sâm*) in Skr., seem to add to the pronoun the force of "here," "same," or "self." **Me** is radically different from *I*. Originally it represented the first pers. sing. feminine. It is identical with Bantu *a*mi (m,' n'), I or me (properly mine), the prefixed *a* being demonstrative and the sign of the genitive. In Herero, *ami* stands at present both in the nominative (just as the English *me* is also sometimes used for *I*) and in the objective case : *ami me i*, I-I-(shall) go, and *hungira ku ami*, speak to me. In the primitive language 32*a MI* was the conditional *i*-form of 32 *MU*, mother, woman, and signified mother here, or woman here, I or me.

In Sanskrit the primitive form has been preserved in the verbal suffix -mi = I : *as*-mi (Lith. *es*-mi, Goth. *i*-m, Engl. *a*-m) = I am.   In mâm (ma-*am*, abbr. mâ), as in *aham* (*a*-h-*am*), the original *i* is lost.

The Hebrew *ani* (*an*-ni), I, is also probably identical with me (*MI*).

WE (*KHI*)

is the natural corresponding plural of *I;* primitive form 9*a KHI*. In *we*, Swed. *wi* or *vi*, O. Sax. *wi*, Germ. *wi-r*, the original radical vowel has been preserved.   We is derived from *I* by a stronger or aspirated pronunciation, just as the Herero plural *o*vi- (6 *KHI*) has been formed from the singular *o*tyi- (4 *KI*).   Bopp indeed says, " Der plural der ersten person ist vom singular stammhaft verschieden, weil das Ich eigentlich keines plurals fähig ist.   Denn es gibt nur Ein Ich."   Quite true, if it could be proved that *I* (Skr. *aham*) had, from the beginning, the abstract meaning which it has now.   But I believe philologists are at present pretty well agreed that in no case language commenced with abstracts.   Besides, the meaning of the first person singular can, in Bantu, methodically be traced to have been "man here, person here," or, in the original feminine gender, "mother here, woman here."   This removes the difficulty at once.   If *I* means "man here," there is no reason why there should not be a corresponding plural, signifying "men here." And this corresponding form has been preserved in the shape of *we*, *wi*, *vi* (for the primitive *KHI*).   It is interesting to observe that in Konde (Bantu) the word has assumed exactly the same form as in English, namely, we-*pa* = we-near = we-here, present, the demonstrative Bantu particle *pa* denoting nearness, hence also presence. And in Herero we meet with the Danish form *vi* (we) in *m*bi (*im*-vi), originally the plural *we*, but at present in use for the singular *I : mbi tare* (orig. that we look, but at present) that I look, just as *tu tare*, that we look, is also used for that I look, or let me look ; *tu pa o*, give me, please ; properly, give us, please.

The parallel form in Skr. is *vayam* (*ve* + *am*).   Vayam, in accordance with the law of the primitive plural, is properly a strengthened form of *aham*.   But it is more especially the dual (radically identical with the plural) which corresponds to *aham* in every particular, inasmuch as both the singular *aham* and the dual *âvâm* appear to have the primitive or Bleek's article prefixed to them, which is not the case in the plural *vayam :*—

*aham (i-*hi-*am)* = this man here, self, **I** ;
*ávâm (i-*vi-*am)* = these men here (them)selves, we (two) ourselves ;
va*yam* (**vi**-*am*) = men here (them)selves, we.

US (*KHU*).

Though the subjective *we* and the objective *us* are at present totally different in sound, neither consonant nor vowel betraying the remotest relationship, yet they appear to be radically one, *us* being the absolute (9 *KHU*), and *we* (9a *KHI*) the conditional form of the same root. That the primitive root of **us** is 9 *KHU* appears to be plain from the Goth. *ugkis (ugk(u)is)*, us two, *igqvis*, you two. The dual form of the second person is evidently only a modification of that of the first person. From the two forms we can easily reconstruct the primitive form. Taking from the first person *ugk-* and adding the *v* or *u* of the second, we have *u-gku*, primitive form *khu-KHU* (9) = *these MEN* = we or us, the initial *u* (*khu*) being the primitive or Bleek's article. The radical *s* in Goth. *unsis*, *u*s, is only a weak trace of the stronger consonant *gk* or *gq* (*kh* or *khh*). The nasal in *unsis*, Germ. *uns*, seems to be inorganic, and the ending *-is* probably means, like *-is* in *veis*, (we) " selves."

The difference thus between the plural pronoun of the first person *us* (*khu-KHU*) and that of the second person *you* (*KHU*) seems to consist simply in this, that the first person is emphasised by the primitive article, which is wanting in the second :—

khu-KHU = *u-***gku** = *u-***s**(**u**) = *u***s** = these men (absolute) = **us** ;
KHU = **you** = men (absolute) = you.

Us and *you*, therefore, stand in a similar relation to each other as Tshuana **ro**-*na* or **tsho**-*na* (= *THU* = *KHU*), we, us, and **lo**-*na* (= *THU* = *KHU*), you. The ending *-na* is demonstrative.

The Herero form for *us* is *tu* (= *THU* = *KHU*), which, in some instances, is also, as in Tshuana, pronounced *tyu* or *tshu*, *e.g.*, *tu-ende* (irregular imperative), go, which is generally pronounced *tyu-ende* or *tshu-ende*, literally (that) we go, or (let) us go.

F

THOU (*KU*).

Thou, Lat. *tu*, Gr. σύ, Germ. *du*, is a variation of the primitive form 7 *KU* (Bantu *u* = thou, *ku* = thee), and means simply man, person (absolute). The labial *v* (*w*) in Skr. *tvam* is properly *u :* *tvam* = *tu-am*, thou. The objective *thee* seems to be an abbreviation of A.-Sax. *thec*, O. Sax. *thic*, Goth. *thuk*, probably a contraction of **thu**-*ik*. The original full form and meaning of *thee* appears to be *KU-iki* = *TU-iki* = thou-self, thyself. The natural plural of **thou** is

YOU (*KHU*),

which literally means men, persons (absolute). Skr. **yû**-*yam* (*KHU* + *am*). The vowel *e* (*i*) in the nominative *ye* (O. Dutch *ghi*) signifies "here, present : "—

$$KHU = \text{men (absolute)} = \text{(you) men} = \text{you} ;$$
$$KHI = \text{men here, (ye) men here} = \text{ye} ;$$

KHI being applied in the first and also in the second person, so that *ye* and *we* appear to be only variations of the same primitive root (9*b KHI*).

In the Skr. dual *yuvâm* (*u*-**v**(*u*)-*am*, *u-KHU-am*) the initial *u* (*yu*) appears to be the primitive or Bleek's article, the radical *u* being absorbed in *â :*—*yuvâm* (you two) = *khu-KHU*(-*am*) = *uKHU* (-*am*) = *these MEN*, these very (two) men, *i.e.* you two.

HE (*KA*),

and its modified form *she*, appear to be identical with Bantu *a* (*ka*), *e*, *ye* (*ke*), **e**ye (cf. Skr. *a*-**y**-*am*, this one), he and she—all variations of the primitive conditional form 7*b KA* = man there = **he** or **she**. The neuter

IT (*KI*),

Goth. *ita*, O. Germ. *iz*, N. H. Germ. *es*, Dutch *het*, Skr. *it*, is perhaps identical with the Bantu neuter form *tyi* (Herero), *si* (*isi-*) in Kafir, *ki* (Kongo), *se* (Tshuana), *ez-* (Mpongwe). Primitive form 4 *KI* = *it*, the living one, animal, but also generally *it*, the thing, place, &c., the initial *i* being probably (as in the Zulu prefix *isi-*) the primitive or Bleek's article.

THEY (*KHA*),

A.-Sax. **thâ**, Goth. **tha***i*, seems to be the natural plural of *he* (*KA*), namely, the conditional form 9*b* *KHA* = men there, though it is possible that the absolute form 3 *KHA* (living ones) may have coalesced with it. It may also be that in 9*b* *KHA* a conditional *a*-form of 6*KHI* (= *THI*) is included.

CHAPTER X.

PRONOMINAL TABLES—THE PRIMITIVE PRONOMINAL SYSTEM RESTORED.

SUCH is the wealth of pronominal forms in Bantu, especially in Herero, that an attempt to restore the primitive pronominal system, comprising the formative prefixes and suffixes of the noun and the pronouns of universal language, ought not to be regarded as hopeless. I have therefore ventured to draw its outlines in the Introduction to my English-Herero Dictionary, and at the end of this chapter similar tables will be found, more complete in so far as they contain the conditional as well as the absolute forms whose characteristics have been explained in Chapter VII.

In the restored pronominal system of Bantu—*which I hold to be the primitive pronominal system of universal language*—there are thirty-three absolute and at least ten conditional forms, thus altogether forty-three. (See the appended tables.)

After what has been said in the preceding chapters on the nature, laws, and original meaning of the pronominal roots, Tables I. and II. will, on the whole and in their outlines, be clear and explain themselves. The forms in **thick type** have in some shape or other been preserved in Bantu, either as formative prefixes of the noun or as pronouns, in most cases as both; those printed in *ITALIC CAPITALS* are hypothetical.

Table III.—The table of the Herero prefixes and pronouns shows that of the forty-three original pronominal forms nearly thirty can still be traced in Herero. There are two or three forms about the identification of which I am not quite sure. *Omi-* IV. may be identical with 23 *PI-MI*, but as *omi-* only occurs as corresponding plural of *omu-* III., it may possibly be a phonetic variation ("umlaut") of the latter form. Also the Nano plural *o*vi- (in *o*vi-ta, bows, plur. of ŭ-*ta*, bow) may not be identical with 24 *PHI*, but likewise an "umlaut" of u-, *o*ŭ- (*o*vu-) XIV. (25 *PU*). Nor is it quite certain that the original form 27 *PHU* has coalesced with *o*u- (*ubu*) XIV. This uncertainty, however, does not interfere with the fact that these three forms, viz., 23 *PI-MI*, 24 *PHI*, and 27 *PHU*, actually existed in the primitive language.

The prefix o- I. seems to be a blending of the primitive noun or pronoun ŭ (7 *KU* = man, person) and the secondary article *a* : *a*-u (*a*-*KU*) = o = *the* person, *the* he (she). Originally o- I. was probably the singular of the sexual dual form *o*mu- (*KU-MU*) I., hence we find it prefixed as a kind of article to proper names and to the names for father (o-*tate*, o-*ihe*) and mother (o-*mama*, o-*ina*), who, considered separately, could, of course, in the beginning of the language, not have been represented by a dual form. The plural *o*o- II. which corresponds to the singular o- I. is probably a contracted demonstrative form of the XIV. prefix *o*u- (9 *KHU* = men, persons), identical with the corresponding separate pronoun *o*ŭ*o* XIV. = they (orig. men, persons, absolute). *O*o- II. (9 *KHU*) would therefore appear to be the original and legitimate plural of o- I. (7 *KU*). Cf. the form *o*o- XIV. (9 *KHU*) in Kongo (Bleek's Comp. Grammar, p. 224).

U- I. is evidently the personal (absolute) pronoun u (= person, he, she) in the genitive case, the sign of the genitive (*a*) being affixed to it. Thus, *e.g.*, the literal meaning of u-*a*-*mbangu* (stranger, alien) is he-of-the separation (om-*bangu* = difference, separation), or the separate one. *O*v- II. (plur. of u- I.) is a demonstrative form of the genitive pronoun v' (ve, va, separate form *o*wo, *o*vo) II.: *o*v-*a*-*mbangu* = they (or those)-of-the separation, *i.e.*, strangers.

It will be noticed that in the Herero objective pronoun 2nd. pers. sing. ku, the radical *k*, lost in the subjective u, has been preserved. This *k* in *ku* must not be mistaken for a remnant of the preposition *k*(*u*). *Me ku sutu*, for example, is not *me k'*u *sutu* (I-to-thee-pay), but, in analogy with all the other objective pronouns, none of which has a preposition, *me* ku *sutu*, I-thee-pay. So also in the Zulu *a-ke* (of him), his, her, the *k* appears to me to be radical; thus not *a-k*-e (of-of-him), but *a*-ke (of him). Bantu *KU* signified originally both thee and him, and *MU* thee (feminine) and her, but when the original meaning (KU = man, person, MU = mother, woman) became lost, KU and MU were employed, without distinction of gender, respectively for *thee* and *him, her : me ku sutu,* orig. I-man-pay, at present, I-thee-pay (male or female); *me mu sutu,* orig. I-woman-pay, at present, I-her or him-pay.

The objective pronoun of the 1st. pers. sing. *m* or *n* (see "Me" in my English-Herero Dictionary) appears to be a mutilated form of (*a*)*mi* (*32a MI*), I.

Table IV. will require a more detailed explanation.

The Hottentot (Nama) Pronominal Forms Reviewed.—In comparing the pronominal roots in Bantu and Hottentot, special caution is needed against the danger of being misled by mere similarity in form and sound. Superficially viewed, we should be tempted to give to most of the Hottentot forms a different place from what they occupy on Table IV. *Sa-rum,* we two, *e.g.,* seems to be nearer 17 *TU-MU* than to 8 *KU-MU.* But we learn in Bantu that in the first and second person only the gutturals *k* and *kh,* and the labials *m* and *mh* are possible, as only these can represent living beings. Thus if the modern pronouns of the first and second person appear with such consonants as *t, d, r, v, b,* or *n,* we know that these sounds are not original, but modifications of *k, kh,* or *m, mh.* In the third person there is the possibility of *t* or *p* being the original consonant, though it will probably be found that in the Hottentot, Semitic, and Aryan families all the primitive forms (on Table IV.) from 10 *TA* till 27 *PHU* are lost, at any rate as far as the personal pronoun is concerned. A few of them may indeed still be recognised as pronominal particles, prepositions or adverbs, as, for example, English *by,* which in Chapter V. we identified with 19 *PA,* but as true pronouns they seem to have altogether disappeared, except in Bantu, where of the said seventeen primitive forms about half the number has been preserved.

Surveying, in the light the study of Bantu affords, the whole of the Hottentot pronominal domain (suffixes of the noun and pronouns), we observe that the primitive compound form 8 *KU-MU* (= Nama *sa*-**khum**, we two) has been admirably preserved here, perhaps better than in any other language. For in the Arabic **hum**, Æthiop. **humu** (they), originally the same as *sa*-**khum** (and *sa*-**kum**, we), the guttural has been changed to a spirant. But most of the Hottentot pronouns are terribly mutilated, so much so that they appear to be the very opposite of those Bantu forms with which we venture to compare them. But it is just this absence of similarity of sound which strengthens our position. The fact is, some of the present Bantu and Hottentot prefixes, suffixes, and corresponding pronouns represent only *half* the original compound form. Now, whilst in the prefix-pronominal Bantu family the *second* half, as a rule, has been preserved, we find in the suffix-pronominal Hottentot the *first* part retained. In other words, in prefix-pronominal and in suffix-pronominal languages the pronouns are identical with the prefixes and suffixes of the noun. Now, it is a rule that a compound pronominal root in its capacity as prefix or suffix is reduced to a monosyllable. Here lies the secret : the dissyllabic prefix naturally loses the *first*, and the suffix the *second* syllable. Thus 2 *KA-MA*, as prefix in Bantu, will, for brevity's sake, throw off the first member, and assume the form of (*KA*)**MA**——, whilst the same primitive form, as suffix in Hottentot, will drop the second syllable, and survive in the shape of ——**KA**(*MA*). Now let the Hottentot suffix **ka** and the Bantu prefix **ma** be joined together, and we have the full primitive form 2 *KA-MA* restored. I quote from the Introduction to my English-Herero Dictionary, p. xiv.:—" If we compare the Khoi-khoi (Hottentot) nominal suffixes with the Bantu prefixes, we observe that in the former the *first part* of the full form exists whilst the second part is dropped (-**kha** or -**ka** instead of *KA-MA*), and that in the latter (Bantu) the *second part* of the full form has been retained, whilst the first syllable has been elided (**ma**- instead of *KA-MA ;* **mu** instead of *KU-MU*), as, for example :—

Herero—o*me-ho* (*KA-MA-iho,* the pair of) eyes ;
Hottentot—*mu-*ka or mu-kha (*mu-KA-MA*), masc. dual, two eyes (from *mu,* to see) ;

and we observe further that, as in Bantu, so also in Hottentot, the *first syllable* of the originally compound form reappears in the corresponding demonstrative pronoun :

NOUN.

Bantu—	(*ka-*)**ma**-*iho,* eyes ;
Hottentot—	*mu-*ka(-*ma*), two eyes.

DEMONSTRATIVE PRONOUN.

Bantu—   *in(i)*ga . . these (orig. two) ;
Hottentot—   *(ne)*ka . . (or *ne*-kha), these two.

For brevity's sake, *KA-MA,* as prefix in Bantu, naturally dropped its first, and, as suffix in Hottentot, its second syllable.   It is as if in one museum the head and front part of some curious animal were found, and in another the back part and tail.   The head is, of course, very unlike the tail, but if both parts are brought together, the whole animal is restored.   So the Hottentot dual suffix -**ka** or -**kha,** just now quoted, is, viewed in itself, very different from the Bantu prefix **ma**- (dual and plural).   And yet both are originally one.   But in their present state they are imperfect, Hottentot -**ka** being the first, and Bantu **ma**- the second member of the compound primitive form.   Let them be joined together, and their oneness as 2 *KA-MA* is clearly seen.

We observe further that the feminine forms in Hottentot have been derived from the masculine or common gender by modifying either the consonant or the vowel, or both.   *Sa*-**khum,** we two (masc.), for example, is changed to *sa*-**im** (*sa-KIM*), we two (fem.), on the same principle as the Hebrew feminine form hi*a*, she, is derived from hu*a*, he, and the Hausa feminine **ke, ki** (thou), from **kai, ka** (thou, masc.) ;   and the radical *s* in the Hottentot feminine plural *sa*-**so,** you, is only a modification of *k*, as found in the corresponding masculine plural *sa*-**ko** (you), analogous to the consonantal change from *m* to *n* in forming the Hebrew feminine *a*ten, ye, **hen,** they, from the corresponding masculine forms *a*tem and **hem.**

Other important points to be borne in mind here, as, for instance, the shifting of person, number, and case, the easy transition from guttural to dental consonants, &c., we have noticed already in Chapters VIII. and IX.   It is especially the vowel *i* or *e* which affects the guttural, and changes it to *ty, tsh, t, s,* &c.   Thus we have in Herero the pronominal roots *ka, ku,* and (not *ki*, but) *tyi, hi,* just as in Italian *c* (*k*) has become *ch* (*tsh*) before *i* and *e*.   *Xei*-**ku** or *xei*-**ka** is in Nama *they* (masc.).   The feminine is derived from this, like Hebrew hi*a* from hu*a*, by substituting the vowel *i*, and the result is that the *k* is changed to *d* : *xei*-**di** (for *xei-KI*), they (fem.) ; *sa*-**kum**, we (masc.) : *sa*- **si**(*m*), we (fem.) ; whilst in *sa*-**im**, we two (fem.), the consonant *kh* (*k*) is entirely suppressed. The radical *t* in **tit***a*, I, is a changed *k*. The relation of Hottentot **ti** or **t***a* (I) to Hebrew *ano*(**ki**) is the same as that of Xosa (Kafir) *n***di** to Zulu *n***gi** or Tshuana **ki**, I. Now, whilst the vowel *i* is bent on turning a guttural to a dental, *u*, on the other hand, shows the tendency of changing *k* to a labial (cf. English *rough*, ruf, *enough*, enuf) ; hence Hottentot *xei*-**b** (Old Egypt. *entof*, suffix -**f**), he (for *xei-KU*) : but *xei*-**s** (O. Egypt. *entos*, suffix -**s**) she (for *xei-KI.*)

We shall now proceed to review the Hottentot (Nama) forms in detail, as we find them in H. Tindall's " Grammar and Vocabulary of the Namaqua-Hottentot Language."

Tit*a* (affix -**t***a*), I. The root is **ti**, primitive form 7*a KI* = man here, I. *Tita* appears to be a reduplication of *ti*, the *a* in the second syllable being demonstrative and identical with the *a* of other objective pronouns, as **b***a*, him, **s***a*, her. The full form is therefore probably *TI-TI-A* (= *KI-KI-A*) = I-I-there = **ti-t***a* = I-me = I, the Nama thus reversing the order of the Herero *a***mi**-*m***e** = me-I = I (present and future tense).

Sa-**ts** (affix -**ts**), thou (masc.), r. **ts** (*tsa, tsu*) = 7 *KU* = man, person (absolute) ; modified feminine form *sa*-**s** (affix -**s**), thou (fem.) : *sa*-**si** = *sa-KI* = *sa-KU* = person (thou, he or she).

Xei-**p** (*xei*-**b**, suffix -**p** or -**b**), he (masc.), r. **b**(*i*) = *BU* (*BA*), primitive form 7 *KU* (conditional 7*b KA*) = man, person, he ; modified feminine form *xei*-**s** (suffix -**s**), she : *xei*-**s**(*i*) = *xei-KI* = *xei-KU* = man, person, he or she.

Xe(*i*)-**i** (suffix -**i**), it (com. gender), originally *xei-KI*, primitive root 4 *KI*, which is the first member of the common plural *xe*(*i*)-**in** (suff. -**n**, -**in** = 5 *KI-MI*), they. The relative pronoun *hia* (the only one left in Nama) = that, which, who, is probably allied to, or rather radically identical with, the suffix -**i** and the pronoun *xei*. Compare the Herero pronoun **i** (he, she, it), the neuter pronoun **tyi** (it), and its corresponding demonstrative form **hi** (this, that).

Sa-**khum** (affix -**khum**), we two (masc.), r. **khum** (aspirated to distinguish it from *kum*, now in use as plural) = 8 *KU-MU* (sexual dual) ; modified forms : *sa*-**im** (*sa-KIM*), we two (fem.) ; *sa*-**rum** (= *sa-TUM* = *sa-KUMU*), we two (com.).

Sa-**kum**, we (masc.), plural, but originally dual, primitive form

8 *KU-MU*; modified forms *sa*-**si** (*sa-SIM*, *sa-KIM* = *sa-KUMU*), we (fem.) ; *sa*-**da** (*sa*-da*m* = *sa-KAM* = *sa-KUMU*), we (com.).

Sa-**kho**, you two (masc.), abbreviated from *sa*-**khum** = *sa*-**kum** = 8 *KU-MU* (sexual dual) ; modified form *sa*-**ro** (abbreviated from *sa*-**rum** = *sa-TUM* = *sa-KUM*), you two (fem. and com.). *Sa*-**kho** is only a somewhat stronger pronunciation of

Sa-**ko**, you (masc. plur.), from which is derived *sa*-**so**, you (fem. plur.), and *sa*-**du**, you (com. plur.) radically identical with

Xei-**ku** or *xei*-**ka** (suffix -**ku**, *KUM*), they (masc.) and *xei*-**di** (suffix -**ti** or -**di**, orig. *KI*, abbreviated from *KIM* = *KUM*), they (femin.), all modifications of 8 *KU-MU*. In

Xei-**kha** (suffix -**kha** or -**ka**, abbreviated from *KAMA*), they two (masc. and com.) and *xei*-**ra** (suffix -**ra** = *TA* = *KA*, mutilated form of *KAMA*), they two (fem. or com. gender), the primitive forms 2 *KA-MA* and 8*b KA-MA* may have coalesced.

As to the suffixes of the noun, their identity with the corresponding pronouns is self-evident, and, as far as our present purpose is concerned, they do not require a special treatment. In whatever light the suffixes may be viewed, either in primary state as primitive nouns, or as roots arrived at pronominal stage (see Tables I. and II.), nothing can be clearer than that the Hottentot terminations of the noun and the corresponding pronouns are identical.

The Hebrew Personal Pronouns Compared.—It is obvious that the study of the Nama pronominal element throws a good deal of light also on the Hebrew pronouns, which evidently have been shaped and adapted in much the same fashion. As in Hottentot, so also in the Semitic languages, the primitive plural forms (with the exception of perhaps one) are extinct, and forms of the sexual dual, variously modified, have been substituted. The feminine forms are not original, but clearly modifications of the masculine (properly personal) gender —in two cases by vowel-change : *at*, *ati*, from *ata*, thou (person) ; hi*a* from hu*a*, he (person)—and in two others by changing one of the consonants : *a*ten, from *a*tem, ye ; hen, from hem, they. But the dual being not represented in the Hebrew pronoun, there was no occasion for carrying the process of modifying and curtailing so far as in Nama.

We notice that in the Hebrew pronouns, just as in Nama (and indeed in our own languages), only those forms have stood their ground which originally represented living things, namely, pronouns which originally had the consonants *k* (modified *h, t,* &c.) and *m* (modified *n*) : the exchange of *k* (*kh, h, s*) and *t* (*th, d, r*) being equally easy in both languages.

The plural pronouns **hem**, they, and *a*tem, ye, are originally forms of the sexual dual (pair, hence more than one, a number), and closely allied to the sign of the dual (-*aim*) and the plural (-*im*), whose primitive form I hold to be 2 *KA-MA* or 5 *KI-MI* = the two (living) things, or also more than one, a number.

In *ano*ki, I, the primitive 7*a KI* = man here, person present, I, appears to have been well preserved. *Ano*ki is the ground-form of the nominal suffix -i = my, and is radically identical with the Æthiop. suffix -ku = I (*gabar*-ku, I made). But supposing the vowel *u* to be radical, and not a colouring of *i*, there is this difference : the Æthiop. -ku is the absolute form, and means simply *man* (hence he, thou and also I), whilst the Hebrew (*ano*)ki is the conditional form, with the by-meaning (man) *here,* thus more definitely I :—

KU, modified *TU* = man, person (absolute), hence he (she), thou ; *KI*, modified *TI* = man *here*, person *present* = I.

It is not impossible that the strong guttural *ch* in *ana*chnu, we, is the original plural of *ano*ki, and identical with 9*a KHI* = men here, we, analogous to the Gothic *ugkis,* us (two), where, in accordance with the primitive plural law, the stronger consonant *gk* represents "more than one," two or a number of *i*k(i), man here, I :—

Hebrew *ano*ki, I.   *ana*-**ch**(-**nu**), we (-we).
Gothic *i*-**k**(i), I.   *u*-**gk**-*is,* us (two).

But when the primitive plural became obsolete or was deemed wanting in emphasis, the originally feminine plural form *a*nu (33 *MHU*), on losing its definite feminine character, was, for the sake of clearness or emphasis, added ; so that possibly the fuller form and literal meaning of the double pronoun *ana*chnu may be not *ana-KI-NU, ana-KI-MHU* (7*a* + 33) = I-we, but *ana-CHI-NU* or *ana-KHI-MHU* (9*a* + 33) = we (com. pers. and masc.) -we (feminine) = "we here-we," the prefixed *ana*- being demonstrative and inorganic.

An analogous case of two originally distinct genders blending into one form we have in Herero *ami-me* = I, and *ami-n*dyi = I, forms in which two genders, the common personal and the originally feminine, combine : the original meaning of *ami-me* and *ami-n*dyi being I (femin.) -I (com. pers.)—a double *I-I*, just as *ana*-ch-nu appears to be a double emphatic *we-we*, in which two originally distinct genders amalgamate.

The other form for I, *ani*, from which the verbal suffixes are derived, is probably not a contraction of *anoki*, but the originally feminine form 33*a MI* (Skr. -mi, Engl. me, Bantu *ami*, Hebr. *a*-ni (*an-MI* = *an-NI*, *a*-ni), I (orig. femin., but afterwards com. gender). In Herero, a prefixed *n* regularly changes *m* to *n*. The fact that in Hebrew the simple form of the verbal suffix of the first person singular is not -*i*, but -*ni*, is certainly in favour of the assumption that the nasal in *ani* is not demonstrative, but radical.

There is ground to believe that in an earlier stage of Hebrew, when the distinction of gender was still observed also in the first person, the forms *ani*, I, and *anu*, we, corresponded to each other as feminine singular and plural; whilst *an-KI*, I, and *an-CHI* (the first part of *anach*-nu) were in use as singular and corresponding plural for the masculine or common personal gender :—

<table>
<tr><td>I. Pers. Sing.</td><td>I. Pers. Plur.</td></tr>
<tr><td>*an*-ki (prim. r. *KI*) = person *here*, I (masc. and com. personal).</td><td>*an*-chi (prim. r. *KHI*) = persons *here*, we (masc. and com. personal).</td></tr>
<tr><td>*a*(*n*)-ni (prim. r. *MI*) = female *here*, I (feminine).</td><td>*a*(*n*)-nu (prim. r. *MHU*, absolute) = females, we, us (feminine).</td></tr>
</table>

*A*tā, thou, modified *at* or *ati*, fem., appears to be only a variation of the objective **ka**, both forms being radically identical with the primitive pronominal root 7 *KU* = man, person. We have remarked already that the exchange of *k* (*kh*) with *t* (*th*), or even a labial, can still be traced in the Bantu pronoun. Such an interchange was, in the beginning of language, impossible. *TU*, for *KU* (living one, person), would have meant an erect dead one, a statue, a raised one ; and *PU* a flying one, an airy one, a spirit. But when by degrees the special characteristics and original powers of the consonants faded away, and only expediency and euphony were consulted, the consonantal interchange between the three different organs of speech came into play—first, it would seem, in the domain of the pronoun, and afterwards also in the verb, especially in the Semitic languages. " Je weiter die sprachen von ihrem ursprunge sich entfernen, desto mehr gewinnt die liebe zum wohllaut an einfluss, weil sie nicht mehr in dem klaren gefühl der bedeutung der sprach-elemente einen damm findet, der ihrem anstreben sich entgegen stellt " (Bopp).

As we mentioned before, the plural forms *a*tem (Arabic *an*-tum), ye, modified fem. *a*ten, appear to be adapted from the sexual dual form 8 *KU-MU* = human pair, hence ye (two), or ye generally. The Arabic has preserved the original *u*, which at the same time shows that the primitive form of *a*tā (thou) and of ka (thee) was something like (*an*)*TU*, *KU* (Herero ku, thee). For the first member of *a*tem (*a*-te-m, *an*-tu-m) is evidently identical with *a*ta, just as ke in ke-m (you) and the objective ka (thee) are the same.

In hu*a*, he, of which *a*ta (thou) and ka (thee) are only variations, we find the primitive *u* of 7 *KU* (man) uncoloured, as also in the Arabic plural hum, f. hunna, they, identical with the blunted Hebrew forms hem, f. hen, they. The primitive form is 8 *KU-MU*, they (pair), more than one person, hence a number, they, and the terminal *u* is preserved in the Æthiop. humu, homu (= hem, hen, they), as also in the Hebrew verbal suffixes -mo, -amo, -emo, them. The feminine form hi*a*, she, is derived by vowel-change from hu*a*, he, as *a*t(i), thou (fem.) from *a*ta, thou, (masc.), Nama di (they, fem.) from ku (they, masc.), sa-im (we two, fem.) from sa-khum (we two, masc.). In the Pentateuch the masculine (originally personal) hu*a* is, with some rare exceptions, common gender, standing for both *he* and *she*, like the personal Bantu u (he, she) and ku (thee, masc. and fem.) : an archaism which in itself alone affords sufficient evidence for the high antiquity of the books of Moses.

General Remarks.—Taking a general survey of the pronominal forms in the Bantu, Aryan, Semitic, and Hottentot families, as represented on Table IV., we observe the following distinctive features and peculiarities in their relation to the common original stock.

In Bantu, the primitive correspondence between singular and

plural has been wonderfully well preserved, also the *forms* of the sexual dual, whilst the *idea* of the dual, except in one case, has been lost, the originally dual forms being now used for the singular and plural. Some original feminine forms are still extant, but they have assumed a common personal and local meaning. Real grammatical gender is, therefore, wanting in the present state of the Bantu languages, no effort having been made by the ancestors of the African nations to keep it alive by substituting conventional feminine forms derived from the common personal gender, as has been done in the Aryan, Semitic, and other families. The personal, neuter, and local meaning are at present the chief features of the Bantu prefixes and pronouns.

The Aryan nations have, in all the three persons, retained the primitive natural plural, whilst few, if any, traces seem to be left of the sexual dual. For the Aryan dual is merely a modification of the plural : in Gothic and other idioms it is evidently, as Bopp has pointed out, a composite consisting of the plural pronoun and part of the numeral two, meaning literally we two, ye two, as Gothic *vi-t* (we two), Lith. *yu-du* (ye two), &c. Also in Sanskrit the dual seems to be radically identical with the plural. The original feminine forms, sing. and plur., *MU* and *MHU*, &c., have been preserved, as, *e.g.* in Skr. *-mi*, I, Engl. *me*, and plur. Skr. *nas* (us), Lat. *nos* (we, us), but the original feminine meaning is lost. Later the feminine was formed from the masculine (or common personal) by change of consonant, as Engl. *she* from *he*, or in other ways.

In the Semitic languages the original correspondence between singular and plural is, except in one or two cases, extinct, forms originally belonging to the sexual dual being in use now for the plural. A few primitive feminine forms have been preserved, but their signification as such has been lost. The feminine of the third person singular is formed from the masculine or personal gender by changing the vowel *u* to *i*.

The Hottentot family, too, has lost the primitive correspondence between singular and plural, but has made the most of a few retained forms of the sexual dual, which have been modified by aspiration, abbreviation, or change of consonant and vowel, to serve as plural and dual pronouns. The feminine is derived from the masculine or personal gender by consonantal and vowel changes.

THE PRIMITIVE PRONOMINAL SYSTEM RESTORED.

TABLE I.—ABSOLUTE FORMS.

Roots in Primary State as Primitive Nouns.

(Forms in thick capitals extant in Bantu.)

SINGULAR, common, personal, and masculine.	SEXUAL DUAL, male-female, couple, pair.	PLURAL, common, personal, and masculine.
Living things.		
1 **KA**, living thing.	2 **KA-MA**, living pair.	3 **KHA**, living things.
4 **KI**, ,, ,,	5 **KI-MI**, ,, ,,	6 **KHI**, ,, ,,
7 **KU**, ,, ,,	8 **KU-MU**, ,, ,,	9 **KHU**, ,, ,,
Dead things.		
10 *TA*, dead thing.	11 *TAMA*, dead pair.	12 *THA*, dead things.
13 **TI**, ,, ,,	14 **TI-MI**, ,, ,,	15 *THI*, ,, ,,
16 **TU**, ,, ,,	17 **TU-MU**, ,, ,,	18 **THU**, ,, ,,
Waving things.		
19 **PA**, waving thing.	20 *PA-MA*, waving pair.	21 *PHA*, waving things.
22 *PI*, ,, ,,	23 **PI-MI**, ,, ,,	24 *PHI*, ,, ,,
25 **PU**, ,, ,,	26 **PU-MU**, ,, ,,	27 *PHU*, ,, ,,
Feminine gender.		
28 **MA**, mother, female.		29 *MHA*, mothers, females.
30 **MI**, ,, ,,		31 *MHI*, ,, ,,
32 **MU**, ,, ,,		33 **MHU**, , ,,

THE PRIMITIVE PRONOMINAL SYSTEM RESTORED.

TABLE II.—ABSOLUTE AND CONDITIONAL FORMS.

Roots arrived at Pronominal Stage.

SINGULAR, *common, personal, and masculine.*	SEXUAL DUAL.	PLURAL, *common, personal, and masculine.*
	Living things.	
1 **KA**, he, she, it.	2 **KA-MA**, he-she, the pair.	3 **KHA**, they.
4 **KI**, he, she, it.	5 **KI-MI**, he-she, the pair.	6 **KHI**, they.
7 **KU**, he, she, it; thou, man, person (absolute).	8 **KU-MU**, he-she, you two, human pair (absolute).	9 **KHU**, they, you, men, persons (absolute).
7a **ki**, man here, I (conditional).	8a **ki-mi**, human pair here, we two (conditional).	9a **khi**, men, persons here (conditional).
7b **ka**, man there, he, she (conditional).	8b **ka-ma**, human pair there, they two (conditional).	9b **kha**, persons there (conditional).
	Dead things.	
10 *TA*, it.	11 *TA-MA*, it-she, the pair.	12 *THA*, they.
13 **TI**, it.	14 **TI-MI**, it-she, the pair.	15 *THI*, they.
16 **TU**, it.	17 **TU-MU**, it-she, the pair.	18 **THU**, they.
	Waving things.	
19 **PA**, it.	20 *PA-MA*, it-she, the pair.	21 *PHA*, they.
22 *PI*, it.	23 **PI-MI**, it-she, the pair.	24 *PHI*, they.
25 **PU**, it.	26 **PU-MU**, it-she, the pair.	27 *PHU*, they.
Feminine gender.		
28 **MA**, mother, female, she.		29 *MHA*, mothers, females, they.
30 **MI**, mother, female, she.		31 *MHI*, mothers, females, they.
32 **MU**, human mother, woman, female, she, her, thou (absolute).		33 **MHU**, human mothers, women, females, they, them, you (absolute).
32a **mi**, mother, female here, I (conditional).		33a **mhi**, mothers, females here, we, ye (conditional).
32b *MA*, mother, female, there, she (conditional).		33b *MHA*, mothers, females, there, they (conditional).

TABLE III.—HERRERO PREFIXES AND PRONOUNS. (*The Roman numbers refer to Bleek's Comparative Grammar.*)

	SINGULAR, *common, personal, and masculine.*	SEXUAL DUAL.	PLURAL, *common, personal, and masculine.*

Originally: Living things.

1 *KA*: o**KA**- XIII. (dimin. and local), pron. **ke**, **ka**, it; **E**-(**KE**) V.

2 *KA-MA*: o**MA**- VI., pron. **e**, they (they two): it.

3 *KHA*: o**ZO**-n- X., pron. **ze**, **za**, they (animals, &c.). Coalesced with 9b *KHA?*

4 *KI*: o**TYI**- VII. (neuter and local), pron. **tyi**, it.

5 *KI-MI*: o**N**-, o**M**- IX., pron. **i**, he, she, it (animal, &c.).

6 *KHI*: o**VI**- VIII., pron. **vi**, they (things, animals, places, &c.).

7 *KU*: o**KU**- XV., pron. **ku**, it; *oku*- (infinitive); o**KO**- XVII. (local), pron. **ku**, it; **ku** sec. pers. sing. obj., thee; **o**- I.

8 *KU-MU*: o**MU**-I., pron. **u**, he, she (man); **u**, *oue*, *ove*, thou; *oye*, thine; **u**- I.

9 *KHU*: o**U**- XIV. (abstract= -head, -hood orig. men), pron. **u**, they, it; **tu**, we, us, (com. gen.); *-etu*, ours; *oo*- II.

7a *KI*: pron. **ndyi**, I (com. gen.); *andye*, mine.

8a *KI-MI*: pron. **i** (in *me*=*ma*-**i**), I (com. gen.).

9a *KHI*: pron. **mbi** (*im*-**vi**, orig. we), I ; *ĕte* (Zulu **ti**, **si**), we, us.

7b *KA*: pron. *eye*, **e**, he, she ; **ye**, him, her; **-e** (other dialects *ake*), his, her.

8b *KA-MA*: pron. **e**, **a**, he or she (in *ma* = *ma*-**a**), Kafir *ma*-**ka**, he, him.

9b *KHA*: o**VA**- II., pron. **ve**, **va**, *owo*, they, them; *-awo*, theirs ; *ov*- II. ; (*ozo*-n-**X**).

Originally: Dead things.

10 *TA*.

11 *TA-MA*.

12 *THA*.

13 *TI*: e(**RI**)- V., pron. **ri**, it.

14 *TI-MI*: o**ZON**- X., pron. **ze**, **za** (**zi**), they (two), they.

15 *THI*.

16 *TU*: o**RU**- XI., pron. **ru**, it.

17 *TU-MU* (coalesced with *ozon*- X.).

18 *THU*: o**TU**- XII., pron. **tu**, they.

Originally: Waving things.

19 *PA*: o**PO**- XVI., pron. **pe**, **pa**, it (local, impersonal).

20 *PA-MA*.

21 *PHA*.

22 *PI*.

23 *PI-MI*: o**MI**-IV. (plur. of *omu*-III.), pron. **vi**, they.

24 *PHI* (? coalesced with) *ovi*- VIII., pron. *vi*, they.

25 *PU*: o**U**- XIV., pron. **u**, it.

26 *PU-MU*: o**MU**- III., pron. **u**, it.

27 *PHU* (? coalesced with) *ou*- XIV., pron. *u*. they, it.

Originally: Feminine gender.

28 *MA*: (incorporated in *oma*- VI.).

29 *MHA*.

30 *MI*: (incorporated in *on*-, *om*-IX.).

31 *MHI*.

32 *MU*: (incorporated in *omu*- I. and III.; o**MO**- XVIII. (local), pron. **mu**, it; obj. pers. pron. **mu**, him, her (com. gen., orig. feminine).

33 *MHU*: pron. sec. pers. plur., subj. and obj. **mu**, **ye**, you (com. gender, orig. feminine); *enu*, your, yours (plur.).

32a *MI*: a**mi**, I, me ; **m**-,**n**-, me (com. gen., orig. fem.).

33a *MHI*: *ene* (Zulu **ni**), ye, you.

32b *MA*.

33b *MHA*.

G